THE FACTORY
SHOP GUIDE

ISBN 0 948965 63 0
ISSN 1350–8784

THE FACTORY SHOP GUIDE

Northern England

✔ Where they are
✔ When they open
✔ What they sell
✔ How to get there

Published by
Gillian Cutress
and Rolf Stricker

Personally researched, written & published by
Gill Cutress & Rolf Stricker
1 Rosebery Mews, Rosebery Road,
London SW2 4DQ
Phone 0181-678 0593 *Fax* 0181-674 1594

1989 The Factory Shop Guide for Northern England
Reprinted January 1990
1990 The Factory Shop Guide for Northern England 1990–91
1992 The Factory Shop Guide for Northern England 1992–93
1994 The Factory Shop Guide for Northern England 1994–95
1996 The Factory Shop Guide for Northern England 1996–97

This is the 62nd edition published in this series

Printed by Garian Press, Huddersfield. Tel: **(01484) 435498**

Contents

Welcome to the fifth edition of our *Factory Shop Guide for Northern England,* the 62nd in our series of guides to factory shopping in Great Britain.

The North continues to offer a marvellous selection of shops, in spite of recent economic setbacks. It now also includes two new factory shop 'villages', each with an excellent variety of products. One of these is on the edge of the Lake District in Kendal, the other in a restored part of Hartlepool. Northern England is well known for a wide variety of footwear, sportswear and top value clothing for the family (especially men). Featured here for the first time are furniture makers who produce upholstered and classical style wooden furniture; one manufacturer offers specially designed chairs for people with spinal disabilities.

Here you can also buy famous name hats, knitwear and underwear, stylish award-winning bags of all kinds in multi-layered canvas normally only stocked in the finest department stores, famous oiled cotton jackets and lots of items suitable for presents, such as art materials and decorative candles. One shop, on the shores of Lake Coniston, included here for the first time, has unique hand-painted table linen, roller blinds and scarves.

With factory shopping it really is a case of 'the more you spend, the more you save' so on large purchases such as three-piece suites, furnishing fabrics and carpets you may well save several hundred pounds. On average you should save a third of the usual price, but sometimes you will come across even greater savings. New readers may like to know that goods can be ends of lines, overmakes, prototypes or 'seconds', in other words goods which failed to meet the most rigorous quality control checks. All represent excellent value for money.

As previous readers are already aware, this book is the result of many miles of travel, looking for and visiting the shops, and assembling details to make shopping trips as carefree and enjoyable as possible, and with clear instructions how to get there.

Whatever you are looking for, factory shopping is fun, and in these days of continuing recession it makes sense to get the best possible value for money, whether you are shopping for everyday essentials, or luxuries at affordable prices.

With sincere thanks to Yanka for her invaluable help with this book.

Alnwick	Sat. Outdoor general.
Ashington	Sat. Outdoor general.
Barrow-in-Furness	Wed, Fri, Sat. Outdoor /indoor general.
Berwick-upon-Tweed	Wed, Sat. Outdoor general.
Bishop Auckland	Thur, Sat. Outdoor general.
Blyth	Tues, Fri, Sat. Outdoor general.
Carlisle	Mon–Sat. Indoor general.
Chester-le-Street	Tues, Fri. Outdoor general.
Cleator Moor	Fri. Outdoor general.
Consett	Fri, Sat. Outdoor general.
Cramlington	Thur. Outdoor general.
Crook	Tues, Sat. Outdoor general.
Darlington	Mon, Sat. Outdoor general.
Egremont	Fri. Outdoor general.
Gateshead	Mon–Sat. Indoor general.
Hartlepool	Thur. Outdoor general.
Hexham	Tues. Outdoor general.
Kendal	Wed, Sat. Outdoor general.
	Mon–Sat. Indoor general.
Keswick	Sat. Outdoor fish and fruit.
Kirkby Lonsdale	Thur. Outdoor general.
Lancaster	Mon–Sat. Indoor general.
	Thur, Fri, Sat. Bric-a-brac/antiques.
	Wed, Sat. Outdoor fresh produce.
Maryport	Fri. Outdoor general.
Middlesbrough	Mon, Thur, Fri. Outdoor general. Mon–Sat. Indoor general.
Morpeth	Wed. Outdoor general.
Newcastle-on-Tyne	Tues, Thur, Sat. Outdoor general at Bigg Market.
	Mon–Sat. Indoor general at Grainger Market.
	Mon–Sat. Indoor general at Grecm Market.
	Sun. Outdoor general at Quayside Market.
Northallerton	Wed, Sat. Outdoor general.
North Shields	Mon–Sat. Indoor general.
Peterlee	Thur am. Outdoor flea market.
Penrith	Tues. Outdoor general.
Redcar	Thur. Outdoor general.
Sedbergh	Wed. Outdoor general.
Shildon	Fri. Outdoor general.
South Shields	Mon, Sat. Outdoor general.
Spennymoor	Sat. Outdoor general.
Stockton	Wed, Fri, Sat. Outdoor general.
Sunderland	Mon–Sat. Indoor general.
Ulverston	Mon, Tues, Thur, Fri. Indoor general.
Whitehaven	Thur, Sat. Outdoor general.
Whiteley Bay	Mon–Sun in summer. Indoor general.
	Mon, Wed, Sat, Sun in winter.
Wigton	Tues. Outdoor/indoor general.
Workington	Wed, Sat. Outdoor general.

Thanks to World's Fair Ltd for allowing us to use information from their 'Markets Yearbook'

Shark Group

Nordstrom House, North Broomhill NE65 9UJ
(01670) 760365

Wetsuits, drysuits, buoyancy aids, inflatable life jackets and accessories for all watersports.

'We sell slight seconds at very competitive prices.'

....

Three miles south of Amble, at the southern end of North Broomhill.

Follow the sign to the Radar pub (on your left if you come from Amble); go behind the pub to the factory.

Open: Mon–Fri 10–4 all year; *also early April–mid Dec:* Sat 9.30–12.
Closed: Three weeks in late July/early Aug; one week late Oct; three weeks at Christmas; Bank Holiday weekends.
Cards: Access, Visa.
Cars: Outside factory.
Toilets: No.
Changing rooms: Yes.
Teas: Meals, morning coffee etc in pub next door.
Groups: No tours but groups of shoppers welcome any time if they arrange in advance.
Transport: Regular bus services to North Broomhill.
Mail order: Yes.
Catalogue: Free on request.

Briggs & Shoe Mines

The Annex, Salutation Hotel LA22 9BY
(015394) 32757

A wide range of sub-standard and clearance footwear of all types for men, women and children.

'All stock made by branded manufacturers.'

See our display advertisement on p. 27

....

Close to the centre of this small town.

From Kendal: get into the one-way system and go around, following signs first to 'Town Centre' then continue towards Kendal again.*

From Keswick: turn left immediately after Jumpers on the left.*

***The shop is behind the large and conspicuous Salutation Hotel on the left, on the first floor.**

Open: *Nov–Easter:* daily 9.30–5.30; *Easter–Oct:* daily 9.30–7.30.
Closed: Christmas Day.
Cards: Access, Connect, Switch, Visa.
Cars: Own coach & car-park.
Toilets: Behind Bertrams Restaurant, 30 yds downhill towards Kendal.
Wheelchairs: Unfortunately no access to first floor shop.
Teas: In Ambleside.
Groups: Coach parties welcome to shop. Drivers can obtain £1 voucher per passenger.
Transport: Bus stops opposite shop. Local transport and buses from further afield.
Mail order: Yes.
Catalogue: Pleased to supply by mail order items in stock if customers know size, fitting and style. Ask for the manager.

3 Ashington Northumberland

Dewhirst Ltd.
Newbiggin Road, North Seaton Industrial Estate NE63 04B
(01670) 813493

Men's wear: quality suits, sports jackets and blazers, trousers, formal and casual shirts, casual jackets, coats. Ladies' wear: blouses, skirts, trousers, dresses, fashion jackets and blazers, suits, casual jackets, coats, handbags, shoes. Children's wear: shirts, blouses, trousers, skirts, dresses, jackets, coats, schoolwear.

'Products are high quality famous chainstore slight seconds. Men's suits from £80.'

South-east of Ashington, not far from the Spine Road (A189).
North Seaton Industrial Estate is well signposted from the centre of town and all approach roads. Enter the estate by the large Focus DIY centre and take the first right behind it. The shop is at the far end of the drive, on the right, well signposted.

Open: Mon–Fri 9–5.30; Sat 9–5; Sun 10.30–4.30. Bank Holidays.
Closed: Easter Sunday; Christmas, Boxing and New Year's Days.
Cards: Access, Connect, Switch, Visa.
Cars: On site, outside shop.
Toilets: No.
Wheelchairs: Ramp, easy access.
Changing rooms: Yes.
Teas: In town.
Groups: No factory tours, but shopping groups welcome; please phone first.
Transport: Ashington town mini service bus stops at factory on request. Bus nos. 335 (Morpeth–Newbiggin) and 434 (Newcastle–Newbiggin) stop 100 yds away.
Mail order: No.

4 Askam-in-Furness Cumbria

K Shoes
James Street LA16 7BA
(01229) 462267

Extensive range of shoes, sandals, boots, slippers and trainers including a wide selection of footwear from *Clarks, Dr Martens, Hi-Tec, Merrell, Puma* and many other famous brands. Good choice of handbags and gifts.

'Average of 30% saving on normal high street prices for perfect shoes. Also wide range of K Shoes discontinued lines and slight substandards for men, women and children. Self-select store but trained staff on hand to measure feet and give assistance if needed.'

Askam is 6 miles north of Barrow. Shop is in centre of Askam near station.
From the south: take Barrow-in-Furness road to Dalton-in-Furness (A590); at mini-roundabout at end of town go straight, up hill for Askam (A595).*
From the north (Workington, Sellafield, Muncaster, Ravenglass Railway): follow A595.*
*Turn off A595 (Workington–Dalton road) in Askam by station. Go over level crossing and straight into James Street. The drive to shop is 50 yds on right, just after K Shoes factory complex.

Open: Mon–Fri 10–5.30; Sat 9–5; Bank Holidays 10–5.
Closed: Christmas, Boxing and New Year's Days. Easter Sunday.
Cards: Access, Switch, Visa.
Cars: Free parking within factory complex and adjacent to the shop.
Toilets: Yes.
Wheelchairs: Easy access.
Teas: In town.
Groups: Free tour of the large adjoining factory available for groups by advance arrangement. Coach parties welcome; concessions for drivers and organisers. £1 voucher per passenger towards purchases.
Transport: Any bus or train to Askam-in-Furness then walk.
Mail order: No.

Errington Reay & Co (Bardon Mill Pottery)

Tyneside Pottery Works NE47 7HV
(01434) 344245

Good selection of large traditional salt-glazed garden pots and domestic storage jars, strawberry and herb pots etc.
'Bargain seconds normally available.'

··

In the middle of the village of Bardon Mill.

Turn south off the A69 (major Newcastle–Hexham–Carlisle road) to Bardon Mill. The tall square chimney of the kiln is clearly visible opposite the road to the station. Follow signs to the car-park.

Open: Seven days 9–5. Please phone to confirm times.
Closed: Weekends from October–Easter.
Cards: No.
Cars: Park behind shop: signposted.
Toilets: Ask if desperate.
Wheelchairs: Fairly steep cobbled path.
Teas: In Bardon Mill.
Groups: No.
Transport: Trains to Bardon Mill from Carlisle and Newcastle.
Mail order: No.

Factory Carpets and Factory Beds

Tundry Way, Chainbridge Industrial Estate NE21 5SJ
(0191) 414 5887

Large range of quality plain and patterned tufted carpets in all yarns and mixes. Axminsters and Wiltons, shadow pile, berbers, twists, underlay, gripper rods etc. In other premises opposite (0191 414 6331): beds and mattresses of all sizes; sofa beds, guest beds; headboards.

'Roll ends and samples always available. Free fitting locally on most carpets.'

··

Immediately south of Tyne between the A1 & Scottswood bridge.

From A1 Western Bypass of Newcastle: turn on to A695 for Blaydon (south of river). Go under approach to old river bridge; take first left for 'Chainbridge Industrial Estate'. The Factory Shop Centre is on left after you cross next bridge.

From Blaydon on A695: go under A1 Western Bypass, take first left into Chainbridge Industrial Estate. The Factory Shop Centre is on right just after left bend.

From Newcastle station: take A695 west. Pass long Vickers factory, go left over Scotswood bridge. After bridge, take first left, go under Scotswood bridge, take first left to Chainbridge Ind. Est. The Factory Shop Centre is on left after you cross next bridge.

Open: Mon–Sat 9–5 (Thur 9–7); Sun and Bank Holidays 10–4.
Closed: Christmas, Boxing and New Year's Days.
Cards: Access, Visa, Eurocard.
Cars: Own car-park.
Toilets: Yes.
Wheelchairs: Easy access.
Teas: Own café.
Transport: Many buses from Gateshead and Newcastle.
Mail order: No.

Factory Fabrics

Tundry Way, Chainbridge Industrial Estate NE21 5SJ
(0191) 414 4515

Vast range of fabrics for curtains, furnishing, upholstery, loose covers etc, including leading designer names and department store clearance stock and over-runs. Curtain lining, tapes, and accessories. Curtain-making service.
'Perfects, seconds and remnants sold at discounted prices.'

Immediately south of the Tyne between A1 and Scottswood bridge.
  From A1 Western Bypass of Newcastle: turn on to A695 for Blaydon (south of river). Go under approach to old river bridge; take first left for 'Chainbridge Industrial Estate'. The Factory Shop Centre is on left after you cross next bridge.
  From Blaydon on A695: go under A1 Western Bypass, take first left into Chainbridge Industrial Estate. The Factory Shop Centre is on right just after left bend.
  From Newcastle station: take A695 west. Pass long Vickers factory, go left over Scotswood bridge. After bridge, take first left, go under Scotswood bridge, take first left to Chainbridge Ind. Est. The Factory Shop Centre is on left after you cross next bridge.

Open: Mon–Fri 10–5 (Thur 10–7); Sat 9–5; Sun and Bank Holidays 10–4.
Closed: Christmas, Boxing and New Year's Days.
Cards: Access, Visa.
Cars: Own car-park.
Toilets: Yes.
Wheelchairs: One step; easy access.
Teas: Own café.
Groups: Groups of shoppers welcome.
Transport: Many buses from Gateshead and Newcastle.

McIntosh's Factory Shop

Tundry Way, Chainbridge Industrial Estate NE21 5SJ
(0191) 414 8598

Large selection of bedding including duvet covers, quilts, bedspreads, pillows, mattress covers, baby bedding; ready-made curtains, net curtains; cushion covers, towels, tea cosies, tablecloths, dusters, dishcloths etc.
'Wide range of perfects and slight seconds.'

See our display advertisement opposite

Immediately south of the Tyne between A1 and Scottswood bridge.
  From A1 Western Bypass of Newcastle: turn on to A695 for Blaydon (south of river). Go under approach to old river bridge; take first left for 'Chainbridge Industrial Estate'. The Factory Shop Centre is on left after you cross next bridge.
  From Blaydon on A695: go under A1 Western Bypass, take first left into Chainbridge Industrial Estate. The Factory Shop Centre is on right just after left bend.
  From Newcastle station: take A695 west. Pass long Vickers factory, go left over Scotswood bridge. After bridge, take first left, go under Scotswood bridge, take first left to Chainbridge Ind. Est. The Factory Shop Centre is on left after you cross next bridge.

Open: Mon–Fri 10–5 (Thur 10–7); Sat 9–5; Sun and Bank Holidays 10–4.
Closed: Good Friday, Christmas, Boxing and New Year's Days.
Cards: Access, Switch, Visa.
Cars: Own large car-park.
Toilets: Yes.
Wheelchairs: One step, but assistance given.
Teas: Own café.
Groups: Groups welcome to shop.
Transport: Many buses from Gateshead and Newcastle.
Mail order: No.

You spend about
1/3 OF YOUR LIFE
in the bedroom

We have got everything to make it more comfortable and attractive at truly amazing prices. We are convinced you will leave satisfied and shop with us again.

Some of our bargains include quilts from £5.99, duvet covers from £9.99 and heavy grade towels from £1.99. Our very reasonably priced bedspreads, pillows, mattress covers, baby bedding, ready-made curtains, tablecloths, tea cosies, dusters, dishcloths etc. will make your day. Then relax in our very own coffee shop.

Open: Mon, Tues, Wed, Fri 10–5, Thur 10–7; Sat 9–5; Sun & Bank Holidays 10–4

McIntosh's Factory Shop Tundry Way, Chainbridge Industrial Estate (0191) 414 8598

Blaydon &

Carlisle

The Factory Bedding and Fabrics Shop
Atlas House, Nelson Street
(01228) 514703

OUR READY MADE CURTAIN DEPARTMENT IS NOW MORE THAN DOUBLE THE SIZE!

The new escalator will carry you effortlessly to our fabric department on the first floor.

Examples of our amazing prices are ready made curtains from £10.99 a pair, curtain tracks from £4.99 each, cotton satin from £4.99 per metre and curtain lining from £1.50 per metre. Here you will also find ready made bedding, duvet covers, quilts, bedspreads, pillows, mattress covers, cushion covers, towels, a huge selection of sheeting, curtaining, upholstery service and a make-up service. Coffee shop opening soon.

Open: Mon–Fri 10.30–5.30; Sat 9–5; Bank Holidays 10–4.

See our entries 8 and 12

The Factory Shop Guide for Northern England

Burberrys

Kitty Brewster Trading Estate NE24 4RC
(01670) 352524

Trench coats, jackets, trousers, shirts; dresses, coats, skirts, sweaters; bags, umbrellas and accessories.

··

On the west side of Blyth.
   From A189 (Spine Road): turn on to A193 for Blyth. Pass Asda on right and go left at second roundabout into Kitty Brewster Trading Estate.
   From Blyth town centre: follow signs to 'A193 & Ashington/ North'. As you leave town, turn right into Kitty Brewster Trading Estate: shop is in first building on right.

Open: Mon–Thur 10–3.30; Fri 10–3; Sat 9–12.30.
Closed: Phone to check for Bank Holidays and Christmas.
Cards: Yes.
Cars: Outside shop.
Toilets: No.
Wheelchairs: One sizeable step to medium-sized shop.
Changing rooms: No.
Teas: In Blyth.
Groups: Groups of shoppers welcome.
Transport: Local buses from Newcastle, North Shields, Whitley Bay Metro.

Claremont Garments

Ennerdale Road, Kitty Brewster Trading Estate NE24 4RF
(01670) 351195

Ladies' wear: lingerie, swimwear, casualwear (bodies, leggings etc), dresses, blouses, skirts, trousers, and tailored suits, coats and jackets. Schoolwear: boys' trousers and shirts; girls' skirts and shirts. Boys' wear: a limited range of casual shirts and trousers.

'All garments are leading chainstore perfects, seconds or ends of lines, and are offered at greatly reduced prices.'

··

On the west side of Blyth.
   From the A189 (Spine Road): turn on to A193 for Blyth. After two pedestrian lights turn left at mini-roundabout, following sign to Kitty Brewster Trading Estate.*
   From Blyth town centre: follow signs to A193 & Ashington/ North. As you leave town, turn right into the Kitty Brewster Trading Estate. at mini-roundabout.*
   *Take first left: shop is 200 yds on right.

Open: Mon–Fri 9–4.30; Sat 9.30–2.30.
Closed: Bank Holidays.
Cards: Most major credit cards.
Cars: Own car-park.
Toilets: In Asda.
Wheelchairs: One small step to medium-sized shop; assistance given.
Changing rooms: Yes.
Teas: In Asda.
Groups: Shopping groups welcome, but large groups please phone first.
Transport: Local buses from Ashington, Blyth, Morpeth, Newcastle.
Mail order: No.

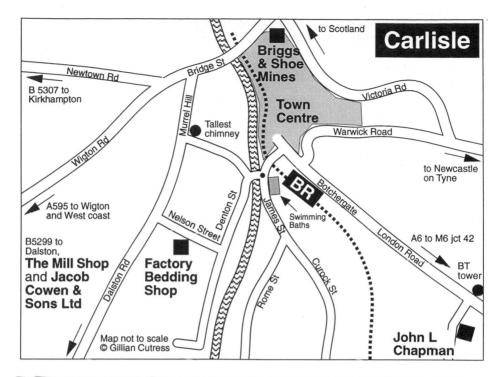

Map not to scale
© Gillian Cutress

Briggs & Shoe Mines

Drovers Lane CA3 8DT
(01228) 819315

Wide range of clearance and sub-standard footwear for all the family. Self selection with expert help and advice available. Small range of clothing and sports apparel.

'Family footwear by famous makers at clearance, reduced or sub-standard prices.'

See our display advertisement on p. 27

Near river bridge north of town centre.
   Follow directions to any town centre car-park. Briggs & Shoe Mines can be found 50 yds from the Civic Centre (Carlisle's tallest building), diagonally opposite the police station.

Open: Mon–Sat 9–5.30 (Tues 10–5.30); Bank Holidays 10–5.
Closed: Christmas Day.
Cards: Access, Connect, Switch, Visa.
Cars: Numerous car-parks in town centre.
Toilets: Yes.
Wheelchairs: No steps, easy access.
Teas: Many cafés in town centre.
Groups: Shopping groups welcome, please contact manager to book. £1 reduction per member of a coach party on purchase.
Transport: Bus stop about 200 yds away outside town market hall.
Mail order: Yes.
Catalogue: Pleased to supply items in stock if customer knows size, fitting and style. Ask for shop manager.

The Factory Bedding and Fabrics Shop
Atlas House, Nelson Street, Denton Holme CA2 5NB
(01228) 514703

Large selection of ready-made bedding: duvet covers, quilts, bedspreads, pillows, mattress covers, baby bedding; ready-made curtains, net curtains; cushion covers, towels, tea cosies, tablecloths, dusters, dishcloths etc. Huge selection of sheeting, curtaining, upholstery fabrics. Make-up service.
'Wide range of perfects and slight seconds.'

See our display advertisement on p. 13

On the south-west side of town, off the road to Dalston.

From Dalston (going north on B5299): pass Calden Hospital on left then turn right immediately before pedestrian lights into Nelson Street. Shop at end of four-storey mill, about 400 yds along.

From other directions: follow signs to station/Motorail terminal. Do not enter station but go into town between two arches like castle (The Citadel). From city centre, follow signs 'West'. Cross Victoria Viaduct to roundabout (baths on left). Take road to Workington; cross bridge, fork left, take fourth right (Nelson Street). Shop on corner of second turning on left.

Open: Mon–Fri 10–5.30; Sat 9–5. Bank Holidays 10–4.
Closed: Good Friday; Christmas, Boxing and New Year's Days.
Cards: Access, Connect, Switch, Visa.
Cars: Outside shop.
Toilets: No.
Wheelchairs: Easy access to spacious shop, but assistance given for first floor.
Teas: Own coffee shop.
Groups: Groups welcome to shop.
Transport: Buses from Woolworths to Morton/Denton Holme; get off by Co-op.
Mail order: No.

Jacob Cowen & Sons Ltd.
Ellers Mill, Dalston CA5 7QJ
(01228) 710205

Cotton and synthetic fibre products: cushion, soft toy and pet bed stuffing; polyester quilt wadding; braided soft fluting for curtain tiebacks, piping etc. Oil absorbent pads, cotton-wool balls, discs and rolls. Cotton wadding for padding, polishing and re-upholstery.
'We sell only perfects but at considerable discount from normal retail prices.'

South-east of Dalston by the river.

From Carlisle on B5299: go through Dalston then turn left just before BP petrol (signposted to Durdar/M6).*

From south on B5299: shortly after you enter Dalston, go right just after BP petrol.*

*Take second left then go right at the sign to Jacob Cowen (just before 'weak bridge' sign).**

From M6 exit 42: follow signs to Dalston directly from the exit roundabout. When you reach Dalston, take first right (dead end sign) then go right after 30 yds into the drive of Jacob Cowen.**

** Factory is at the end of drive.

Open: Mon–Thur 9–1 and 2.15–4.45; Fri 9–1.
Closed: Friday; Christmas–New Year; most Bank Holidays but please phone to check if open.
Cards: Access, Visa.
Cars: Ample parking outside factory.
Toilets: Ask if necessary.
Wheelchairs: Easy access, no steps.
Teas: In Dalston village.
Groups: Shopping groups welcome, but please phone first.
Transport: Trains to BR Dalston from Carlisle. Buses from Carlisle and Penrith.
Mail order: Yes.
Catalogue: No.

John Chapman Ltd.

Gallery House, Harraby Green Business Park
CA1 2SS
(01228) 514514

Huge collection of award winning fishing bags, shooting and hunting bags, travel and shoulder bags, in multi-layered canvas, tweeds and tartans with leather trim and solid brass fittings.

'These bags are found only in the finest department stores and speciality shops worldwide. Bags of classic British design and rugged construction, built from all British raw materials to last a very long time. First quality, test models, some seconds and used bags available.'

....

In beautiful old mill at southern edge of Carlisle, close to British Telecom tower.

   From town centre: take A6 south. By BT tower (large transmitting aerial with satellite dishes), go right (20 yds before Esso station on left) to Harraby Green Business Park (signposted).*

   From M6 exit 42: take A6 into Carlisle. By BT tower, take first left after Esso petrol station (on right).*

   *Immediately go sharp left betwen two rows of terraced houses to Gallery House (signposted).

Open: Mon–Thur 9–5; Fri 9–3.
Closed: Bank Holidays; Christmas–New Year. Please check for spring and summer holidays (usually Spring Bank Holiday week; last week July, first week August).
Cards: No.
Cars: Outside.
Toilets: Yes.
Wheelchairs: Two small steps to shop.
Teas: Local pubs; teas in town.
Groups: Suitable for small shopping groups only.
Transport: Bus nos. 61, 62 south from town. Get off at Harraby Green/BT tower.
Mail order: Yes.
Catalogue: Please phone or write for free catalogue.

The Mill Shop

Cummersdale Print Works
(01228) 25224

Curtain fabrics and linings. Printed furnishing fabrics.
'All products are substandard or ends of ranges.'

....

About two miles south-west of Carlisle.

   From B5299 (Carlisle–Dalston road): follow signs east to Cummersdale. Go through village, and go left at bottom of valley before river. Shop, clearly signed, is in low building on left.

Open; Mon–Fri 9–4.30; Sat 10–4.
Closed: Please phone to check.
Cards: No.
Cars: Visitors' car park.
Toilets: No.
Wheelchairs: Easy access to medium sized shop on ground floor.
Teas: In town.
Groups: Shopping groups wishing to visit should phone first, mentioning this guide.
Transport: None.

Lili Atkins Home Furnishings

26 Market Street LA5 9JY
(01524) 733542

Co-ordinated designer wallpaper, fabrics and borders, own manufacture and other people's goods to order. Designer accessories, eg lamp shades, cushions and bedlinen.

'Perfects available; clearance lines and seconds at 50% discount.'

In the centre of Carnforth.
    From M6 exit 35: follow signs into Carnforth. In front of Shell petrol on right, go right.*
    Coming south on the A6: in town, go right in front of Shell petrol.*
    *Booths supermarket is on right. Park here and take either walkway through to Market Street. This shop is on this side of the road, opposite the post office.
    Coming north on A6: at traffic lights, go left. Shop is a short distance on right, opposite the post office.
    From the station (on your right): go to traffic lights and cross over main road. Shop is on right, opposite post office.

Open: Mon, Tues, Wed and Fri 9–5; Thur, Sat 9–1.
Closed: Bank Holidays. Check for opening during Christmas period.
Cards: No.
Cars: In Booths supermarket car-park, and take small walkway through to Market Street.
Toilets: Nearby.
Wheelchairs: Access difficult, two steep steps.
Teas: Lovedays tea shop nearby, home made produce.
Groups: No tours; shopping groups 6 maximum.
Transport: Carnforth BR station 2 minutes' walk. Bus service from Lancaster.

Abbey Horn of Lakeland

Units 6a & 6b Holme Mills, Holme LA6 1RD
(01524) 782387

Shoe horns, spoons, spatulas, salad servers, soldiers' mugs, paperweights, bottle openers, corkscrews, walking sticks, all made of ox horn. Also horn ships, brushes, combs.

'All items perfect with prices reduced by 1/3.'

Holme is six miles north of Carnforth, just west of M6, between M6 exits 35 and 36. Company is in industrial estate south of Holme.
    From M6 exit 36: go towards Kirkby Londsale; after 150 yds go right for Holme on A6070. After 2 miles go right for Holme over motorway. In Holme, go left opposite The Smithy pub.*
    From Milnthorpe on A6: turn towards Holme at traffic lights; once out of Milnthorpe, fork right for Holme. In Holme turn right opposite The Smithy.*
    *Continue until you pass mill pond on left and first entrance to industrial estate. Take second entrance after about 200 yds. Park on right in marked spaces. Walk down 80 yds between the units: units 6A and B are on right.

Open: Mon–Fri 9–4.
Closed: Bank Holidays; Christmas–New Year.
Cards: None.
Cars: Small area in front of factory.
Toilets: No.
Wheelchairs: Access to factory tour but not to shop (16 steps).
Teas: Local pub.
Groups: Abbey Horn, established in 1749, is the oldest working horn works and the only one open to public. Factory tours £1 per head. Groups welcome – please call Heather McKellar first.
Transport: Bus no. 55 from Kendal.
Mail order: No.
Catalogue: Only wholesale catalogue.

Kangol Ltd.
Cleator Mills CA23 3DK
(01946) 810312

Range of formal and casual hats for men and women; caps, berets, peak caps; handbags; scarves; golf clothing; streetgear; belts.

'First quality, ends of ranges and slight seconds available. Prices from about £2 to £30.'

About 11 miles south-west of Cockermouth, on A5086 south of Cleator Moor.

From Cockermouth on A5086: go through Frizington to Cleator Moor; at bottom of hill, after The Brook and opposite church, go left into Kangol's drive.*

From Egremont on A5086: go through Cleator, pass Grove Court Hotel on left and turn right before The Brook into Kangol's drive.*

***Shop is on left, clearly signed.**

Open: Mon–Fri 10–4; Sat 9–1.
Closed: Bank Holidays; Christmas and New Year.
Cards: Access, Visa.
Cars: Own car-park; adequate coach parking.
Toilets: No.
Wheelchairs: Easy access to large shop.
Teas: Local pubs.
Groups: No factory tours.
Transport: Whitehaven/ Egremont buses stop in Cleator.
Mail order: No.

Stylish hat as illustrated in the Royal Wedding edition of The Graphic, March 1922

John Countryman & Co. Ltd.

The Rural Workshops, Lake Road
(015394) 41129

Hand-printed tablecloths, napkins, roller blinds, scarves, cushions, tablemats etc. Also picture gallery showing work of local artists: prints and originals.

'On the shore of Lake Coniston. All our designs are unique and exclusive to us.'

Near the lake south-east of village centre.
  From the south on A593: turn right at the first crossing signposted to Gondola Steam Yacht Pier. *
  From Ambleside or Hawkshead: go through the village, over the river and take the first left after the Burmah Petrol Station signposted Gondola Steam Yacht Pier. *
  ***After 1/3 mile go straight instead of turning left for the lake, then follow the signs.**

Open: Mon–Sat 10–5.
Closed: Bank Holidays; Christmas–New Year.
Cards: Not yet.
Cars: Own car-park.
Toilets: In Coniston.
Wheelchairs: Easy access, no steps to medium sized premises.
Teas: At Bluebird Café and many other local places.
Groups: Shopping groups welcome, no need to book.
Transport: Buses from Windermere and Ambleside stop 50 yds away.

Jumpers

Bridge Mill LA6 2HR
(015242) 71071 x 300

Men's and ladies' own brand designer knitwear; embroidered blouses and sweatshirts, socks and separates from this season and last season.

'Perfects and seconds. Prices from £2; up to 50% off normal retail prices.'

Modern brown factory building on the south-west end of Cowan Bridge.
  From Skipton on A65: Jumpers is on the right just as you enter Cowan Bridge.
  From Kirkby Londsale: follow signs to Ingleton and Skipton on A65. About 1.5 miles after river bridge, go through Cowan Bridge and Jumpers is on left.

Open: Mon–Fri 10–4, plus last weekend in Jan, Feb and March; then every weekend April–Sept inclusive.
Closed: Christmas and New Year's Days.
Cards: Access, MasterCard, Switch, Visa.
Cars: Own free car–park.
Toilets: No.
Wheelchairs: Easy access, no steps.
Changing rooms: Yes.
Teas: In town (Kirkby Lonsdale).
Groups: Everyone welcome.
Transport: None.
Mail order: No.

Lonrho Textiles (Accord and Brentfords)

Nelson Way Trading Estate NE23 9JT
(01670) 713434

Large selection of quilt covers, sheets, pillowcases, continental quilts, pillows and towels.

'We sell perfects, seconds and rejects .'

....

West of Cramlington town.

From Blyth or Bedlington: take A189, then A192 to 'Cramlington Industrial Estate'. *

From A1 north of Tyne Tunnel: take A189 going north; pass Cramlington town, take A192 to 'Cramlington Industrial Estate'. *

***Once on A192 continue on to A1068 and turn left. Follow signs to Nelson Way Industrial Estate; factory is first on left.**

From Newcastle: take A6125 or new Western Bypass; go north and branch on to A1068 for Bedlington. Turn off A1068 into Nelson Industrial Estate (signposted); shop is first on left.

Open: Mon–Fri 9–5; Sat 9.30–4.30.
Closed: Bank Holidays; Christmas, Boxing and New Year's Days. Please phone to check Christmas opening.
Cards: Access, Visa.
Cars: In factory car-park inside security gates.
Toilets: No.
Wheelchairs: No steps, easy access to large shop.
Teas: Not locally.
Groups: No guided tours.
Transport: Bus no. 442 (Ashington–North Shields) stops outside factory.
Mail order: No.

Furness Footwear

Long Lane, off Mill Brow
(01229) 462744

Men's, ladies' and children's fashion shoes, both leather and synthetic.

'Vast range of branded footwear from own factory and all over the world. Stock changes daily. Prices from £1 to £100.'

....

Off the A590 south of Dalton-in-Furness.

From town centre, Ulverston and Askam-in-Furness: go towards Barrow-in-Furness at roundabout. Go out of town, pass Burmah petrol station on right, take next left (Long Lane). Shop in second building on right.

From Barrow-in-Furness via A590: pass Furness General Hospital, go straight at roundabout, go right after 500 yds towards Stainton. Shop in second building on right.

Open: Mon–Sat 9–5.30 (Fri late night to 8). Bank Holidays.
Closed: Christmas, Boxing and New Year's Days.
Cards: Access, Switch, Visa.
Cars: Factory car-park.
Toilets: Ask if desperate.
Wheelchairs: Easy access to large shop.
Teas: Hot-drinks machine; sweets, crisps, biscuits on sale.
Groups: Welcome to shop.
Transport: Main Barrow–Ulverston buses stop at shop.
Mail order: No.

Hall & Son – a Lotus Shoes factory shop
6 Blackwellgate DL1 6HL
(01325) 466009

Ladies' court shoes and sling backs, sandals, leather casuals, fashion shoes. Men's city styles, casuals and sandals. Also seasonal footwear such as slippers and ladies' fashion boots. Handbags.

'This is a factory shop belonging to Lotus Shoes. A visit here could be part of a day's shopping trip.'

In the centre of town near the Market Hall (with a large clocktower).

From the top end of the Market Hall: go left of Binns department store and keep going around it. Hall & Son are on the same side of the road, 50 yds beyond Binns.

Open: Mon–Sat 9–5.30.
Bank Holiday Mondays.*
Closed: *Tuesdays after
Bank Holiday Mondays.
Christmas and New Year.
Cards: Access, Switch, Visa.
Cars: Double yellow lines.
Large car-park at lower end of
the Market Hall. Also
Skinnergate.
Toilets: Below Market Hall.
Wheelchairs: Easy access,
some steps to the back of shop.
Teas: In town.
Groups: Coach parties
welcome: please contact
Mrs L Kell.
Transport: About 300 yds
from the main bus stop in
town.
Mail order: No.

The Factory Shop Ltd.
Empire Buildings, Main Street CA22 2BD
(01946) 820434

Clothing and footwear for all the family. Good range of branded bedding, towels, toiletries, pottery, lighting and fancy goods. *Lee Cooper* concession. New fashion concessions department with famous brand names for women.

'Large stock of chainstore items, all at greatly reduced prices. Deliveries of new stock every week to give an ever changing selection.'

In the town centre beside Wyndham School (signposted).

Turn into the side road immediately beside the town hall (with magnificent clocktower) and almost opposite tourist information centre. Go to end of that road and shop is clearly signposted.

Open: Mon–Sat 9–5; *also in
December:* Sunday.
Closed: Bank Holidays;
Christmas, Boxing and New
Year's Days.
Cards: Access, Switch, Visa.
Cars: In factory car-park.
Toilets: Ask if desperate.
Wheelchairs: Easy access
to large shop.
Changing rooms: Yes.
Teas: In town.
Groups: Shopping groups
welcome. For organiser/driver
incentives please phone.
Transport: Buses from
Whitehaven.
Mail order: No.

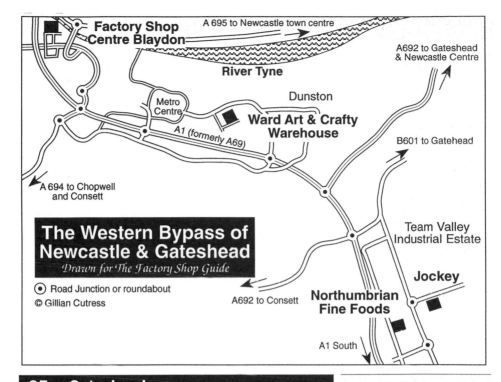

Ward Art & Crafty Warehouse

Halifax Road, Dunston Industrial Estate NE11 9HV
(0191) 460 5915

Art materials; craft products; stationery; children's art and drawing products; pens and markers; paper; school stationery; paints and brushes; art cases; drawing boards; airbrushes; drawing, sketching and painting sundries.

'Many special offers up to 50% off retail price, eg watercolour sets half-price; free videos with drawing sets; briefcases from £9.95; drawing pads from 85p each; artists' brushes from 58p for six etc.'

From the A1 (Western Bypass) going north: pass A692 turn-off into Newcastle but take next exit to Dunston. *

From the A1 going south: pass 'Metro Centre' exit; take next exit to Dunston. *

*Turn downhill towards Dunston. Pass Burmah petrol station on left, go under railway bridge, take first left (Lancaster Road) then take first left again. Shop is 100 yds on left, clearly signed.

From Metro Centre: follow signs to Dunston, pass brewery on right and take next right (Lancaster Road) then take first left. Shop is 100 yds on left, clearly signed.

Open: Mon–Sat 9–5.
Closed: Bank Holidays; Christmas & New Year's Days.
Cards: Access, Switch, Visa.
Cars: In street.
Toilets: By request.
Wheelchairs: Nine steps. Access at rear on request.
Teas: In Dunston or Metro Centre and from take-away van. Sweets and chocolates in shop.
Groups: Shopping groups please book with Karen Carpenter or Carole Creed. Free factory visits for groups of up to 15. Contact John Moreels or Miriam Wright. Sometimes art and craft demonstrations/exhibitions.
Transport: Metro Centre railway station. Bus nos. 745, M8, M7 stop nearby.
Mail order: No.

Jockey

Eastern Avenue, Team Valley Trading Estate NE11 0PB
(0191) 491 0088

Wide selection of men's and ladies' underwear, T-shirts, knitwear, tights, socks; towels, bedding, baby accessories, swim/sportswear (in season).

'Perfects and seconds.'

··

The Team Valley Trading Estate is just off the A1 Western Bypass.

Exit from the A1 to 'Team Valley', NOT 'Team Valley and A692 Consett' (the northern end of the estate). Continue down this dual carriageway to a roundabout signposted to Low Fell (right) and turn right into Eastern Avenue. Shop is on the right in the first building after the first turn-off to the right.

Open: Mon, Tues, Thur 10–4; Fri 10–2.30.
Closed: Please check with company.
Cards: No.
Cars: Own car-park outside shop.
Toilets: No.
Wheelchairs: Easy access to large shop.
Changing rooms: Yes.
Teas: In Low Fell.
Groups: No factory tours. Groups of shoppers welcome but please phone first.
Transport: Bus from Gateshead to Team Valley.
Mail order: No.

Northumbrian Fine Foods (makers of Dunkers)

Dukes Way, Team Valley Industrial Estate
(0191) 487 0070/482 2611

Selection of plain and coated biscuits: plain £1.20/kg, half coated £1.60/kg, fully coated £2.10/kg. Dunkers. Vegetarian ready meals, soups, jams.

··

The Team Valley Trading Estate is just off the northern A1 Western by-pass.

Exit from A1 at 'Team Valley', NOT 'Team Valley/A692 Consett' (northern end of estate). Follow signs to 'Retail World'. At roundabout with Mobil petrol station on right, turn right into Dukes Way. Shop is in silver coloured building 400 yds on right.

Open: Mon–Fri 9.30–1.30.
Closed: Bank Holidays; last week July and first week August; Christmas–New Year.
Cards: None.
Cars: Outside shop.
Toilets: No.
Wheelchairs: Two small steps.
Teas: In Texas and Queensway in Retail World.
Groups: No.
Transport: Bus no. 915 from Newcastle; no. 83 from Gateshead.

Jackson's Landing

Hartlepool Marina TS24 0XM
(01429) 866989

Jackson's Landing is the north-east's only purpose-built factory outlet mall. Well known designer label fashions and household goods within their units.

'Perfect surplus stock and discounted lines. Plus factory seconds all at unbelievably low prices direct from the manufacturers. Up to 60% off normal retail prices on quality brand name goods.'

See our display advertisement inside front cover

In dock area north of town centre.

From A179 southbound: follow signs for town centre and Hartlepool Marina. Jackson's Landing is on the left as you pass the docks.

From the A689 northbound: go through town centre following signs to Hartlepool Marina, go over the railway bridge and Jackson's Landing is on the right past the Heritage Centre.

Open: Mon–Sat 10–6; Sun 11–5.
Closed: Christmas Day.
Cards: Major credit and debit cards.
Cars: Free parking for 2500 cars and 10 coaches.
Toilets: Yes.
Wheelchairs: Automatic doors, lifts, toilets; wheelchairs available.
Changing rooms: Yes.
Teas: Full catering facilities on site.
Groups: Shopping groups always welcome, incentives available; contact centre manager.
Transport: Hartlepool BR station 10 minutes' walk.

Claremont Garments

Howdon Green Industrial Estate, Willington Quay NE28 6SY
(0191) 263 1690

Ladies' wear: lingerie, swimwear, casualwear (bodies, leggings etc), dresses, blouses, skirts, trousers, and tailored suits, coats and jackets. Schoolwear: boys' trousers and shirts; girls' skirts and shirts. Boys' wear: a limited range of casual shirts and trousers.

'All garments are leading chainstore perfects, seconds or ends of lines, and are offered at greatly reduced prices.'

In an industrial estate east of Wallsend, near Howdon Metro station.

From Wallsend: take the A193 to Howdon and North Shields. In Howdon go straight at the traffic lights, then take the fourth right into Howdon Lane. (Fish & chip shop on the corner and large pub 'Bewick Park' opposite).*

From the A19 just north of the Tyne tunnel: take the A193 towards Howdon and Wallsend. After the A19/A193 inter-change, turn left into Howdon Lane (immediately after the first pedestrian crossing).*

*Continue across the level crossing at Howdon Metro Station, take the first left and next left again. Shop is 50 yds on your left through the last door of that building.

Open: Mon–Fri 9–4.30; Sat 9.30–2.30.
Closed: Some Bank Holidays; Christmas, Boxing and New Year's Days.
Cards: Most major credit cards.
Cars: Own car-park.
Toilets: No; nearest in town centre.
Wheelchairs: No steps; easy access to large shop.
Changing rooms: Yes.
Teas: In town centre.
Groups: Shopping groups welcome, but large groups please phone first.
Transport: Howdon Metro station about 300 yds; various bus routes.
Mail order: No.

Daleswear Factory Shop

High Street LA6 3AB
(015242) 42373

High quality outdoor and leisurewear. Fleece jackets, pullovers, pants, accessories etc for adults and children, including *Polartec 200* fleece. *Aquatex* waterproof mountain jackets, overtrousers and salopettes. *Kingsdale* caving oversuits and undersuits, *Gold Flash* tackle, *SRT* bags etc.

'Mostly firsts, competing in standard and design with market leaders, at much lower prices. Also prototypes, seconds, clearance and bargain lines.

Discount 10% (off non-sale items) to anyone showing this guide.'

Ingleton Village is on the A65 between 28 miles north-west of Skipton and six miles south-east of Kirkby Lonsdale.

Follow one-way system up through the village centre. The High Street is up from the square and the shop is next to the Wheatsheaf pub.

Factory Shop may move to Laundry Lane at edge of village, with own car-park, in late 95.

Open: Mon–Sat 9–5 (including Bank Holidays); Sun 9.30–5.00.
Closed: Christmas, Boxing and New Year's Days.
Cards: Access, Switch, Visa.
Cars: Limited High Street parking; main parking at Community Centre.
Toilets: Ask if desperate.
Wheelchairs: Three steps; large shop.
Changing rooms: Yes.
Teas: In Ingleton.
Groups: Shopping groups welcome; group factory tours by arrangement.
Transport: None.
Mail order: Yes.
Catalogue: Free. Sell everything by mail order.

Barbour

Monksway, Bede Industrial Estate NE34 2HF
(0191) 455 4444 (ask for shop)

Oiled cotton jackets, trousers, moleskin shirts and trousers; warm pile linings; corduroy trousers; all made by this company. Also sell sweaters, shirts, hats, bags, quilted jackets and waistcoats.

'All items are factory seconds plus some discontinued lines.'

Next to Bede Metro station and half a mile from south entrance of Tyne Tunnel.

From roundabout at south entrance of tunnel: take A185 dual carriageway towards South Shields; after about 600 yds take first right (soon after dual carriageway ends). Turn left at T-junction, then take first right and right again before second factory. Shop is at the end of this building.

Open: Tues–Fri 10–5; Sat 9–12.
Closed: Mondays; Bank Holidays; first week June; last week July; first two weeks August; two weeks at Christmas. Please phone for exact dates.
Cards: Access, Switch, Visa.
Cars: Own car-park outside.
Toilets: No.
Wheelchairs: Easy access, no steps.
Changing rooms: No.
Teas: Two pubs nearby; teas in Jarrow.
Groups: Coach parties welcome to shop; please contact Mr Heads, mentioning this guide.
Transport: Next to Bede Metro station.
Mail order: No.
Catalogue: Yes.

32   **Kendal**   **Cumbria**   *see map on next page*

Briggs & Shoe Mines
Sandes Avenue LA9 4SG
(01539) 721335

Over 10,000 sq ft sales area with 100,000 pairs of boots and shoes for all the family. Wide range of sports and walking footwear. Handbags, socks, accessories etc.

'Half of shop sells reduced-price major branded, sub-standard and clearance lines, including K Shoes directly from K factories in Kendal. 60 major international brands at regular price. Measurement and fitting by qualified staff.'

See our display advertisement above

Within the town centre.

Sandes Avenue is the northern link in the busy one-way system round town. From the A6 (Stricklandgate), the main road which goes from south to north through Kendal: turn right towards Penrith. This large conspicuous shop is on the right, 25 yards from the corner.

Open: *Summer:* Mon–Sat 9–7; Sun 11–5. *Winter (Nov–Easter):* Mon–Sat 9–5.30; Sun 11–5. Bank Holidays 10–5.
Closed: Xmas Day, Easter Sun.
Cards: Access, Connect, Switch, Visa.
Cars: Own car-park; multi-storey behind shop (car-park ticket gives you reductions on footwear). Free coach park 120 yds away (with bus washing!).
Toilets: Yes.
Wheelchairs: Easy access to huge shop.
Teas: Café next door.
Groups: Coaches welcome, mention this guide. Parties receive £1 voucher per person towards purchases.
Transport: 150 yds from Kendal BR; Kendal mini-link bus network.
Mail order: Pleased to supply items in stock if customers know size, fitting and style.

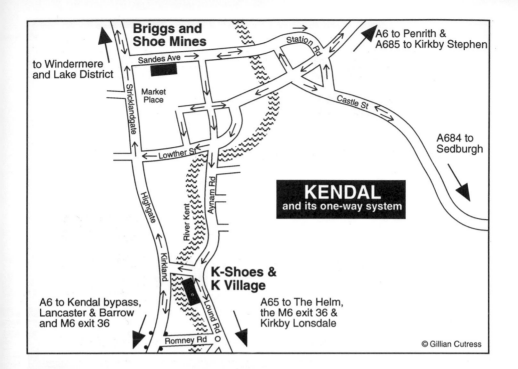

Map labels:
- Briggs and Shoe Mines
- A6 to Penrith & A685 to Kirkby Stephen
- Station Rd
- Sandes Ave
- to Windermere and Lake District
- Stricklandgate
- Market Place
- Castle St
- A684 to Sedburgh
- Lowther St
- Aynam Rd
- River Kent
- Highgate
- **KENDAL** and its one-way system
- Kirkland
- K-Shoes & K Village
- A6 to Kendal bypass, Lancaster & Barrow and M6 exit 36
- Lound Rd
- A65 to The Helm, the M6 exit 36 & Kirkby Lonsdale
- Romney Rd
- © Gillian Cutress

---

33 Kendal Cumbria *see map above*

K Shoes Factory Shop, Sports Factory and Baggage Factory

Netherfield LA9 7DA

(01539) 721892

Extensive range of quality shoes, sandals, boots, walking boots, slippers, trainers, handbags, luggage, sports clothing, sports equipment, outdoor clothing, accessories and gifts.

'Exciting new K Shoes factory shop. Great savings averaging 30% less than in the high street from K Shoes, Clarks, Springers, CICA and other famous brands. Self-select store with trained staff to measure feet and give assistance where needed.'

In K Village, on the A65 on south-east side of town.

From town centre: take A6 south signposted to M6. When you see signs to A65, follow these until you see K Village on right. Entrance at far end of complex: follow signs to shop.

From south via A65: as you come into Kendal, clearly signposted complex and shop are on left shortly after you reach river (on left).

From A591(T) northbound (Kendal bypass): take A6 for Kendal and turn right at first traffic lights signposted to K Factories. Take first left after bridge then first left into car-park. (This is quickest way from M6 exit 36.)

Open: Mon–Fri 9.30–6; Sat 9–6; Sun 11–5. Bank Holidays 9–6.

Closed: Christmas Day and Easter Sunday.

Cards: Access, Switch, Visa.

Cars: Free parking at rear of the building (places for disabled drivers).

Toilets: Yes, including for disabled; baby changing facilities.

Wheelchairs: Most entrances and exits have ramps for wheelchairs, & shopping aisles are wide enough for easy access.

Teas: Leith's at the Food Factory Restaurant. Also sandwich bar.

Groups: Coach parties welcome, concessions for drivers and organisers. £1 voucher per passenger towards purchases. Play area for children.

Transport: Ten minutes' walk from town centre or bus route 41/41A.

34 Kendal Cumbria

see map on previous page

K Village

Netherfield LA9 7DA
(01539) 721892

Undercover mall with factory shop units operated by *Jumpers, Crabtree & Evelyn, Dartington Crystal, Denby Pottery, K Shoes Full Price Shop, K Shoes Factory Shop, The Sports Factory, Baggage Factory* and *The Village Gift Shop.*
'Shop at your leisure in undercover shopping mall and visit our unique Heritage Centre.'

See our display advertisement above

On the A65 on south-east side of town.

From town centre: take A6 south signposted to M6. When you see signs to A65, follow these until you see K Village on right. Entrance at far end of complex: follow signs to shop

From south via A65: as you come into Kendal, clearly signposted complex is on the left shortly after you reach river (on left).

From A591(T) northbound (Kendal bypass): take A6 for Kendal and turn right at first traffic lights signposted to K Factories. Take first left after bridge then first left into car-park. (This is quickest way from M6 exit 36.)

Open: Mon–Fri 9.30–6; Sat 9–6; Sun 11–5; Bank Holidays 9–6.
Closed: Christmas Day.
Cards: Access, Switch, Visa.
Cars: Large free car and coach park outside shop; spaces for disabled drivers.
Toilets: Yes, also for disabled; baby changing facilities.
Wheelchairs: Most entrances and exits have ramps for wheelchairs, & shopping aisles are wide enough for easy access.
Teas: Leith's at Food Factory Restaurant. Sandwich bar.
Groups: Coach parti welcome, concessions for drivers and organisers. £1 voucher per passenger towards purchases in K Shoes Factory Shop. Play area for children.
Transport: Ten minutes' walk from town centre or bus route 41/41A.

Barker Shoes Factory Shop at Pattinsons
Lupton Court CA12 5JD
(017687) 72016

High quality shoes for men and women. All perfects. Cater for extreme sizes and fittings. All shoes made by Barker Shoes.

'Barkers unique quality at direct factory prices. No rejects.'

This shop is at the rear of Pattinsons Shoes which is on Main Street in the centre of Keswick.

Open: Mon–Sat 9–5.30. Bank Holidays.
Closed: Phone to check Christmas and New Year opening.
Cards: Access, Switch, Visa.
Cars: In car-park opposite.
Toilets: In town.
Wheelchairs: One step to ground floor shop.
Teas: Lots of pubs and cafés.
Groups: Small shopping groups welcome.
Transport: Any bus to Keswick.
Mail order: Yes.
Catalogue: Free.

Standfast
Caton Road LA1 3PB
No phone in shop.

Seconds in printed fabrics, including many well known designer names for curtains and upholstery (cottons, linens, chintz and sateens). Also sell small pieces suitable for cushions or patchwork.

Nearly a mile north of the town.
From Lancaster: follow signs to the M6 (northbound). This takes you along the A683 (Caton Rd). Pass the clock-tower on the left, then the company is 100 yds on the left, with the name clearly displayed.
From M6 exit 34: follow the signs to Lancaster. Company is about a mile on your right, immediately past Shell petrol station.
Please do NOT park inside main gate – hinders emergency access.

Open: Mon–Fri 9.30–1; Sat 10–12.30
Closed: Bank Holidays; Christmas–New Year.
Cards: None.
Cars: Special car-park across the road.
Toilets: Yes.
Wheelchairs: Five steps into shop. You can arrange to go in via the warehouse for easier access.
Teas: In Lancaster.
Groups: No mill tours.
Transport: None.

Colony Country Store
LA12 0LK
(01229) 465099

All kinds of candles: tapers, pillars, decorated, scented, novelty. Many different colours and fragrances. Floral rings, candlesticks, holders, lamps. Textiles, ceramics, placemats, napkins, tablecloths, kitchen accessories (co-ordinating designs/colours). Christmas shop open all year.

'Unrivalled for colour and scent. From 10p–£60 with substantial discounts on firsts and seconds.'

....

On the A590, 2.5 miles south-west of Ulverston on road to Barrow. Look for 'Candle Workshop' signs.

From Ulverston via A590: pass The Anchor on right then go left opposite post office into London Road, just after pedestrian crossing.*

From Barrow on A590: go through Dalton-in-Furness and pass sign 'Lindal' on left. After 400 yds go right into London Road before the pedestrian crossing, opposite post office (at start of town).*

*Go over railway bridge. Shop is on left.

Open: Mon–Sat 9–5; Sun 12–5.
Closed: Christmas and Boxing Days.
Cards: Access, Visa.
Cars: Parking by factory; space for two coaches.
Toilets: Yes, and for disabled.
Wheelchairs: No steps; easy access.
Teas: Chandlers café on site for snacks/full lunch Mon–Sat 10–4.45, Sun 12–4.45.
Groups: See traditional candle-making through shop viewing gallery. Visit grotto where Santa tells fairy tales to animated woodland friends. Groups welcome: prior phone call appreciated.
Transport: Ulverston–Barrow buses each 1/2 hour.
Mail order: No.

Historic town of Maryport

Maryport was for a time the biggest port in Cumberland. It was founded in 1749 by an Act of Parliament promoted by Humphrey Senhouse II, the Lord of the Manor, who named it after his wife Mary. From the eighteenth century onwards the local industry was developed mainly by several powerful families, including the Senhouses and the Curwens. It was in Workington Hall, the ancient seat of the Curwen family, where Mary Queen of Scots, fleeing from her rebellious Scottish subjects, spent her last night of freedom. Another famous incident concerns a local man, Fletcher Christian, who led the mutiny on the Bounty in 1787 on its return trip from Tahiti.

The mining of plumbago, lead and copper had taken place on the western fells for many years, but it was the exploitation of the large deposits of high grade haematite ore on the western fells which eventually brought the greatest economic and social changes. Coal mining was mainly for export, and the local traders soon saw the potential for trade with the New World. Towns and villages grew at a tremendous pace, having attracted people from the surrounding countryside, and from Ireland, Scotland, the Isle of Man and as far as Cornwall.

Thanks to the Tourism Section, Borough of Allerdale.

Grasshopper Babywear Ltd.
Unit 200/19 Industrial Estate CA15 8NE
(01900) 815998

Babywear from 0–2 years. Sleepsuits, pyjamas, rompers, bodysuits, vests, underwear.
'Perfects and seconds.'

....

Just south of the town.
   Turn off the A596 (Maryport–Workington road) when you see the sign to Solway Trading Estate. Take the first left, and the shop is about 100 yds on the right.

Open: Mon–Thur 10–4.
Closed: Bank Holidays. Christmas–New Year.
Cards: No.
Cars: Own car-park.
Toilets: Ask if required.
Wheelchairs: Easy access, no steps.
Changing rooms: No.
Teas: In town.
Groups: No factory tours, but shopping groups welcome.
Transport: Bus no. 300 (Carlisle–Whitehaven) a few minutes' walk.

New Balance Athletic Shoes (UK) Ltd.
St Helen's Lane, Flimby CA15 8RY
(01900) 602850

Running shoes, football boots, hiking boots, basketball boots, tennis and squash shoes, cross trainers, fitness shoes, walking shoes, sports clothing, sports bags.
'First quality as well as seconds sold here.'

....

Off the A596, south of Flimby between Maryport and Workington.
   From Maryport: go south through Flimby, turn left after Armstrong Ltd. *
   From Workington: go north, pass Ectona and turn right after Laing. *
   ***Take first right and New Balance is at end of drive.**

Open: Mon–Fri 9.30–5.30; Sat 9–4. Bank Holidays.
Closed: Christmas, Boxing and New Year's Days.
Cards: Access, Delta, Electron, Switch, Visa.
Cars: Outside shop in factory car-park.
Toilets: In Workington.
Wheelchairs: Easy access to medium sized shop.
Changing rooms: Yes.
Teas: In Workington.
Groups: Parties welcome to shop; please contact Chris Mintoft, mentioning this book.
Transport: Maryport–Workington buses stop outside.
Mail order: No.
Catalogue: Yes.

Engraving of Lancaster dated about 1875

Catalogue Bargain Shop

51 Acklam Road TS5 5HA
(01642) 825925

Huge range of mail order surplus items: clothing, fashions, household, footwear, hardware, furniture, electrical, toys and gifts.

'Large savings from original catalogue prices. Firsts & seconds.'

....

On A1032 south-west of the town centre and south of West Lane Hospital.
   From Darlington on A66: turn right on to A19 south.*
   From Middlesbrough: easiest to take A66 west then turn on to A19 south.*
   From the north on A19 cross the river Tees and A66.*
   ***Pass race course on right; exit for A1130. At the top, go left and immediatley left again (Levick Crescent). At the end (church on right), go left into Acklam Road A1032. Shop is on right shortly after second turn-off to right.**

Open: Mon–Sat 9–5; Sun 10.30–4.30; Bank Holidays.
Closed: Christmas Day.
Cards: Access, Delta, Switch, Visa.
Cars: In side roads.
Toilets: No.
Wheelchairs: No steps; easy access.
Changing rooms: Yes.
Teas: None nearby.
Transport: Bus nos. 21, 22, 24; most Middlesbrough Corporation buses.
Mail order: No.

Dannimac Ltd.

Southbank Road, Cargo Fleet TS3 8BH
(01642) 247794

Ladies' and men's rainwear and casual wear.
'Seconds and discontinued lines.'

....

On the A175 at the eastern end of Middlesbrough centre.
   From A19: take A66 for Middlesbrough and Teesport to roundabout where A171 turns right to Whitby.*
   From town centre: take A175 for Redcar. This takes you on to A66 to Teesport to roundabout where A171 turns right to Whitby.*
   ***Turn right here and left at next roundabout on to A175. Then take first right and immediately go right again on to service road. Shop is at end of this road.**

Open: Usually third Saturday of month 9–11 am, occasionally more often (advertised in local press). Essential to phone first.
Closed: Christmas–New Year.
Cards: Access, Switch, Visa.
Cars: Own car-park.
Toilets: Yes.
Wheelchairs: No access, shop upstairs.
Changing rooms: Yes.
Teas: Canteen open during winter sales.
Groups: For coach party visits to the shop, please contact Mr Hodgson first, mentioning this guide.
Transport: Middlesbrough–Redcar buses go along the main road.
Mail order: No.

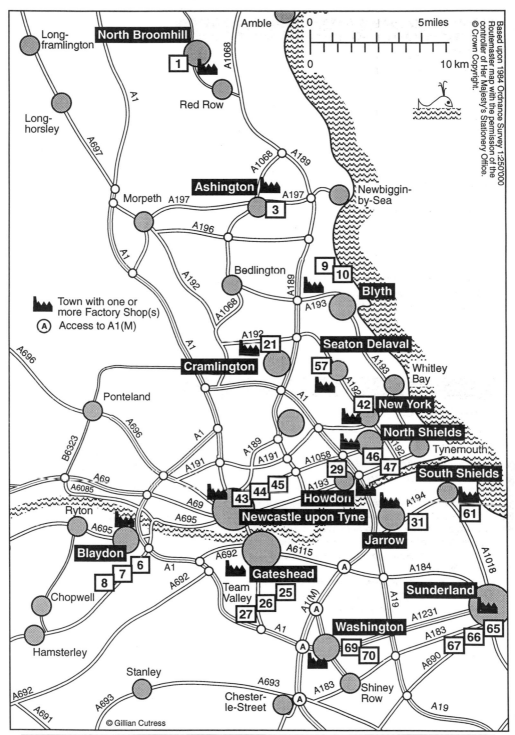

Based upon 1984 Ordnance Survey 1:250 000 Routemaster map with the permission of the controller of Her Majesty's Stationery Office.
© Crown Copyright.

Long-framlington

North Broomhill

1

A1068

Amble

0   5 miles
0   10 km

Red Row

Long-horsley

A1

A697

A1068   A189

Ashington

A197

3

A197

Newbiggin-by-Sea

Morpeth   A197

A196

A1

A192

Bedlington

A1068

A189

9

10

Blyth

A193

Town with one or more Factory Shop(s)

(A) Access to A1(M)

A192

21

Seaton Delaval

Cramlington

57

A193

Whitley Bay

A696

Ponteland

A696

A1

A1

A189

A191

42

A192

New York

A1

North Shields

Tynemouth

B6323

A69

A6085

A69

A191

A1058

A193

29

46

192

47

South Shields

43 44 45

Howdon

A194

61

Ryton

A695

A69

A695

Newcastle upon Tyne

31

Jarrow

Blaydon

6

A1

A692

A6115

(A)

A194

A1018

8   7

A692

Gateshead

Team Valley

25

A184

Chopwell

26

A1(M)

A19

Sunderland

27

A1

(A)

Washington

A1231

65

Hamsterley

A183

69 70

66

67

Stanley

A692

A693

Chester-le-Street

A183

(A)

Shiney Row

A690

A19

A691

A693

© Gillian Cutress

The Factory Shop Guide for Northern England

35

Hobart Rose plc

Middle Engine Lane NE29 8HG
(0191) 258 2233

Soft furnishing manufacturers: made-to-measure curtains, fabrics, bean bags and cushions etc.

'Seconds, samples, ends of line etc sold here at factory prices. Also at Stakeford Lane, Stakeford, Northumberland.'

....

On an industrial estate south-west of New York (and north-east of North Shields).

　From A19 (formerly A1) north of Tyne tunnel: exit on A1058 for Tynemouth. Take next exit and follow signs to New York Industrial Estate. Turn left after about 1/2 mile by the Shiremoor Farm restaurant signposted to West Chirton Industrial Estate. Take the next left into Alder Road: shop is first on right, clearly signed.

　From A191 (Gosforth–Whitley Bay road): turn south on to Norham Road North at roundabout with Vauxhall dealer (Reg Vardy) on near right. Take first right (Middle Engine Lane), then first left (Alder Road): shop is first on right, clearly signed.

Open: Mon–Sat 9.30–4.
Closed: Bank Holidays; Christmas–New Year.
Cards: Access, Visa.
Cars: Outside shop.
Toilets: No.
Wheelchairs: Easy access to medium sized shop.
Teas: Local pubs and cafés.
Groups: Shopping groups welcome, but please phone first.
Transport: Bus nos. X10, X38, 308 from Newcastle; easier by car.

Catalogue Bargain Shop

51 Shields Road, Byker NE6 1DJ
(0191) 265 6033

Huge range of mail order surplus items: clothing, fashions, household, footwear, hardware, furniture, electrical, toys and gifts.

'Large savings from original catalogue prices. Firsts & seconds.'

....

About 1.25 miles east of city centre, off the A193.

　From the south on A167: go over Tyne bridge, pass exit to city but take next exit to A193 signed Byker/Walker. *

　From the north on A167(M): turn on to A193 signed Byker/Walker (large Warner Bros cinema on left). *

　From city centre: follow signs to Byker/Walker/North Shields via A193 and cross the A167(M). *

　*Go over three traffic lights, then the high Byker bridge; go left at first roundabout. Shields Road swings to the right: the shop is on near left corner by next traffic lights.

Open: Mon–Sat 9–5; Sun 10.30–4.30; Bank Holidays.
Closed: Easter Sunday; Christmas Day.
Cards: Access, Delta, Switch, Visa.
Cars: In Roger Street at rear.
Toilets: No.
Wheelchairs: One step.
Changing rooms: Yes.
Teas: Several snack bars in Shields Road.
Transport: Bus nos. 12, 39, 40 to Shields Road, or Metro to Byker Station.
Mail Order: No.

Delta Outdoor Equipment

*Unit 14B, Airport Industrial Estate, Kenton Bank Foot
NE3 2EE*
(0191) 286 1137

Weatherproof and waterproof jackets; tent awning repairs
and alterations. Also thermal clothing with some styles for
all ages.

*'Firsts and seconds sold here. Special offer prices on ends
of lines.'*

....

Off the A696 just west of A1 Western Bypass.

**From the A1 Western Bypass: turn off to A696 but take the
turn to 'Airport Industrial Estate'. At next roundabout go right to
Industrial Estate and right again after Texas DIY. Then take first
left, first right, next left and next two right turns. Shop straight
ahead at top.**

Open: Mon–Fri 9–5; Sat 10–3.
Closed: Bank Holidays;
Christmas–New Year.
Cards: No.
Cars: Outside shop and in
road.
Toilets: No.
Wheelchairs: One wide step;
easy access.
Changing rooms: No.
Teas: Opposite, or in Tesco.
Groups: Shopping groups
welcome – please phone first.
Transport: Kingston Park
Metro station and buses
close by.
Mail order: Yes.

Palatine Products

Whickham View NE15 6UM
(0191) 241 0170

Wide range of beds in all price ranges: from cheaper
firm top bases to top quality sprung-edge, pocketed sprung
bases. Range of mattresses. Three-piece suites. Household
furnishing accessories, eg headboards, pillows.

*'All items first quality. Genuine manufacturer selling at
"unbeatable" trade prices.'*

....

About two miles due west of Newcastle city centre.

**From western bypass (A1): at large junction with A69
(Carlisle turn-off), take A69/A6115 towards Newcastle. At
first roundabout, go right into Denton Road (A191).***

**From central Newcastle: take A6115 for Carlisle. After about
two miles, at roundabout where A696 crosses, go left into
Denton Road (A191).***

***At next roundabout go left, Whickham View (B1311). Shop
is in huge factory, half a mile on left.**

Open: Mon, Wed, Sat 9–5;
Thur–Fri 9–5.30.
Closed: Please phone about
Bank Holidays;
Christmas–New Year.
Cards: Access, Visa. Credit
facilities.
Cars: Own car-park.
Toilets: No.
Wheelchairs: Ramp to front
door.
Teas: Coffee available.
Groups: Groups welcome to
free factory tour if arranged in
advance – please contact
Mike Hughes.
Transport: Bus nos. 30, 31,
38, 38B from outside Odeon in
city centre.

Fashion works at the Discovery Museum

Many museums around the country have fashion exhibits arranged in chronological order. But Newcastle's Discovery Museum (0191 232 6789) is the first to take a thematic approach in their recently opened permanent Fashion Works costume gallery.

One of the eight departments concentrates on the production of fibres, dyes and fabrics; another tells a scenic story, based on a nineteenth century poem 'The Song of the Shirt', showing a poverty stricken seamstress hand-working intricately decorated dresses for a rich Victorian woman. The history of retail fashion is demonstrated with a Victorian scene in Fenwick's of Newcastle, and more modern fashion outlets are also represented.

One department deals with image, exploring our habits of colouring our hair and changing the shade of lipstick and finger nails, and another sets out to prove that even fashion can be environmentally friendly, with a collection of clothing made from unbleached cottons, fabrics produced without pesticides and without exploitation of workers.

On a highly practical note, there is a department which specialises in maintenance, which will show you how to look after precious fashion purchases. It tells you, for example, how to care for silk, and explaina what can make woollies end up fitting only the cat, or as polishing cloths!

With thanks to Tyne and Wear Museums for this information

Finding your way there

Preparing directions for finding the shops takes an inordinate amount of time. What might seem on the surface like a straightforward undertaking can become very complicated and very time-consuming, especially in city centres, in heavy traffic and when you simply cannot avoid the almost inevitable one-way system. How simple life was when you could go *up* and *down* each street!

Recognising that some shoppers prefer to navigate by maps, while other people find it much easier to follow verbal directions, we aim to give accurate details in the clearest way possible. Densely built urban areas present the greatest challenge to preparing directions (so that anyone can track down each shop from any direction). We assume that the reader has basic maps and a road atlas of the country.

We are constantly taken aback by the frequency with which roads, road numbers, road signs, roundabouts and one-way systems change, and how often petrol stations alter brand. If you notice such changes, we will be very grateful if you will let us know.

We need your help

We are a very small and very personal venture and we have gained a great many friends around the country over the last ten years. Precisely because we are so small, we need your help. Mainline publishers organise expensive and impressive publicity campaigns; we rely on personal contact. This is especially important when it comes to shops in this book. They need to know that the book works for them, that they benefit by appearing in it.

So, each time you visit a factory shop in this book, PLEASE TELL THE FACTORY SHOP MANAGER THAT YOU USE THE FACTORY SHOP GUIDE.

Bargain Baggage Factory Shop
Bugatti House, Norham Road NE29 7HB
(0191) 258 4451

Branded luggage by *Pierre Cardin, Gino Ferrari*; business accessories and attaché cases in quality leather and man-made fibres. Wide range of small leather goods and handbags. Shopping bags, beach bags.

'Perfects, seconds and ends of lines at well below high street prices.'

....

On the north-east side of North Shields.

From A19 (formerly A1): turn on to A193 for North Shields. At next roundabout go left for Tynemouth (A1058). After 0.4 miles turn left immediately after Bugatti House. Shop is about 80 yds on left.

On A1058 from Newcastle: cross over A19 and take next exit; turn right at the top and company is 1/2 mile on right. Turn right immediately before Bugatti House: shop is 80 yds on left.

Open: Tues 10–2; Wed–Fri 10–3. *Also* Sat, Sun in *December:* phone for details.
Closed: Monday; Christmas–New Year.
Cards: Access, Diners, Visa.
Cars: Outside shop.
Toilets: No.
Wheelchairs: Easy access, no steps.
Teas: In North Shields and Tynemouth.
Groups: Shopping groups please write to Christine Quinn to book.
Transport: Percy Main metro station. Buses for Newcastle and Whitley Bay. Bus nos. 42 and 55 from North Shields go past; 305 and 308 coast road buses stop outside Formica factory, then 3 minutes' walk.
Mail order: No.

Midas House Furnishers
Norham Road NE29 8JD
(0191) 257 6997

Manufacturers of a large range of exclusive settees and chairs. Also made to measure. Extensive selection of fabrics and leather. Specially designed chairs created for people with spinal disabilities.

'Always bargains; showroom clearance. 12 months' interest free credit. Prices from £799 for full three-piece suite; up to £1200 for leather.'

....

On the north-east side of North Shields.

From the A19 (formerly A1) north of Tyne tunnel: exit on to A1058 for Tynemouth. Take next exit and follow signs to New York Industrial Estate. Shop is about 500 yds on left, set back from the road.

From A191 (Gosforth–Whitley Bay road): turn south into North Norham Road at the roundabout with Vauxhall dealer (Reg Vardy) on near right. Shop is about 1/2 mile on the right, set back from road.

Open: Mon–Sat 10–4; Sun 12–4. Bank Holidays.
Closed: Christmas Day.
Cards: No.
Cars: Outside shop.
Toilets: Yes.
Wheelchairs: Two steps; easy access to large shop.
Teas: In North Shields.
Groups: No factory tours.
Transport: Percy Main metro station. Buses for Newcastle and Whitley Bay. Bus nos. 42 and 55 from North Shields go past; 305 and 308 coast road buses stop outside Formica factory, then 8 minutes' walk.
Mail order: Yes.
Catalogue: Yes.

North Shields

There are a number of quayside shops in North Shields where you can buy fresh fish.

The recorded history of North Shields begins in 1225, when the prior of Tynemouth built for his workers, to the east of the present fish quay, 27 huts (or sheels, from which the name of the town derives). The settlement was soon to include mills, bakehouses, a fish quay and a brewery. In the fourteenth century, however, a Royal edict gave Newcastle mercantile supremacy, and an Act in 1530 forbade the loading and discharging of ships anywhere on the Tyne except Newcastle, although salt and fish were exempt. During several centuries North Shields and Newcastle upon Tyne vied with one another for trade: the people of North Shields rebelled against these restrictions, while the burgesses of Newcastle did not want to lose their monopoly of trade on the Tyne. Newcastle considered North Shields 'a town where no town ought to be'.

With pressure from local MPs concerned about the poor navigability of the Tyne, the Tyne Improvement Commission, established in 1850, remedied the situation with improvements which helped develop the fishing and related industries in North Shields. Although many of these industries are now in decline, the town remains the most important fishing port between Hull and Aberdeen.

Its exposed position on the mouth of the Tyne was the scene of many shipwrecks and deaths. Piers have now made the area much safer, but the local RNLI boat is still periodically called upon to assist at incidents at sea.

A two mile walk around North Shields Fish Quay and the riverside area gives an insight into the town's history and development. From Western Quay you get good views of the fishing fleet. There are about seventy boats in the North Shields fleet, and many boats from other east coast ports land fish in North Shields regularly. The best time to see the fleet being unloaded is early in the morning.

*With thanks for these details to the
North Tyneside Council.*

Calvert's Carpets

Standard Way, Darlington Road DL6 2XA
(01609) 779189

Large range of quality tufted carpets in all yarns and mixes made here. Large selection of room-sized roll ends, many at less than trade prices. Patterned Axminsters and Wiltons; cords.

'Clearance lines, seconds and remnants of wide range from cheap cords to heavy Wiltons. Free measuring service. Expert fitting available. See our other shop in Lytton Street, Middlesbrough.'

....

At the northern end of town.

From Darlington go south on A167: as you reach Northallerton, pass first factory on right and turn right by sign 'Industrial Estate'.

From all other directions and the town centre: take the A167 north for Darlington. Go over level crossing, pass Toyota garage then turn left to 'Industrial Estate'. Shop is 80 yds on left.
[Next to CB Home Furnishings, see next entry.]

Open: Mon–Sat 9–5 (Thur to 7); Sun and Bank Holidays 11–4.
Closed: Christmas, Boxing and New Year's Days.
Cards: No.
Cars: Large car-park.
Toilets: Yes.
Wheelchairs: Easy access, no steps.
Teas: In town.
Groups: Shopping groups welcome, but larger groups please phone first.
Transport: None.

CB Home Furnishings

Standard Way, Darlington Road DL6 2XB
(01609) 772916

Continental quilts, pillows, bedding; curtains and accessories, fabrics; pine and metal beds, sofabeds, three-piece suites; bedroom and sitting room furniture. Towels and lace.

'Some seconds and ends of ranges sold here. Everything at competitive prices. See our other shop in North Ormsby Road, Middlesbrough'

....

At the northern end of town.

From Darlington go south on A167: as you reach Northallerton, pass first factory on right and turn right by sign 'Industrial Estate'.

From all other directions and the town centre: take the A167 north for Darlington. Go over level crossing, pass Toyota garage then turn left to 'Industrial Estate'. Shop is 80 yds on left.
[Next to Calvert Carpets, see previous entry.]

Open: Mon–Sat 9–5 (Thur to 7); Sun and Bank Holidays 11 4.
Closed: Christmas, Boxing and New Year's Days.
Cards: No.
Cars: Own car-park
Toilets: Yes.
Wheelchairs: Easy access to very large shop.
Teas: In town.
Groups: Shopping groups welcome, but larger groups phone first.
Transport: None.

Briggs & Shoe Mines

Southend Road CA11 8JH
(01768) 899001

Wide range of shoes for all the family. Self selection, with expert help and advice available. Small range of clothing and sports apparel, accessories, socks etc.

'3,000 sq ft of sales area for family footwear by famous makers, all at clearance, reduced or sub-standard prices.'

See our display advertisement on p. 27

....

South of the town centre.
   From the town centre: take the A6 for Kendal and turn right opposite Shell petrol station (signpost to 'Swimming Baths'), then follow signs to car-park. Shop is adjacent to car-park.
   From M6 exit 40: take A66 east; turn left at roundabout on to A6 for Penrith. Turn left opposite Shell petrol station and follow signs to car-park.

Open: Mon–Sat 9.30–5.30; Bank Holidays 10–5.
Closed: Christmas Day.
Cards: Access, Connect, Switch, Visa.
Cars: By shop or in adjacent car-park.
Toilets: In car-park.
Wheelchairs: Difficult access as 5 stairs to main shop floor.
Changing rooms: No.
Teas: In town.
Groups: Shoppers welcome. £1 reduction per member of a coach party on purchase. Pre-booked meals for parties at Caesar's Restaurant. Driver's gratuity; company pays for coach parking.
Transport: Buses pass by.
Mail order: Yes.
Catalogue: Pleased to supply by mail order items in stock if customers know size, fitting and style. Ask for manager.

Town & Country Manner

Penrith Industrial Estate CA11 9EO
(01768) 890986

Large range of outdoor clothing; country wear and quality classic fashion for all the family. Up to 50" waist, 20" collar for gents, size 30 for ladies. Skirts, trousers and jackets with some exclusive lines. Shoes, boots, socks, waterproofs, workwear and home linens. Mail order ends of lines, one-offs from bargain cloth buys, overmakes and seconds.

'Traditional quality at realistic prices. Most garments made specifically for this shop, including very large sizes to order. Always special offers. Skirts usually under £20; other items up to 40% off.'

....

West of Penrith close to the motorway.
   From town centre: aim for M6/Keswick. At roundabout with Shell petrol station on right, follow signs to Penrith Industrial Estates. *
   From M6 exit 40: aim for Penrith. At first mini-roundabout (Shell petrol station on left), go left following signs to Penrith Industrial Estates. *
   *Go under railway bridge; shop is 200 yds, clearly signed, on left.

Open: Mon–Sat 9–5; Sun 10–5.
Closed: Christmas Day; usually open New Year's Day, please check.
Cards: Access, Visa.
Cars: Own car-park at rear.
Toilets: Yes.
Wheelchairs: One step to large warehouse; assistance gladly given.
Changing rooms: Yes.
Teas: Café opposite and hotel nearby; tea shops in town.
Groups: Shopping groups welcome, larger groups please phone first.
Transport: Penrith station 15 minutes' walk, buses to Penrith.
Mail order: Yes. From brochure range only. Phone 01768 899111, mentioning this guide, for free mail order brochure to view small selection of range.
Catalogue: Free.

Wetheriggs Country Pottery

Clifton Dykes CA10 2DI
(01768) 899122

Traditional hand-thrown terracotta gardenware, earthenware and stoneware for casual dining, kitchen and table. 700 sq ft candle room.

'Museum and history trail of the historic pottery and original working steam machinery. Scheduled industrial monument and the only steam powered pottery in the UK.'

....

A few miles south south-east of Penrith.

From M6 exit 40: turn on to A66 towards Scotch Corner then take A6 towards Shap at next roundabout. *

From Penrith: go south on A6 and cross A66. *

***From this roundabout go for about 3 miles; turn left towards Cliburn. Follow signs to pottery about two miles on the right.**

Open: Seven days 10–5 (*summer* 9–8). Bank Holidays.
Closed: Christmas.
Cards: Mastercard, Switch, Visa.
Cars: Own car-park.
Toilets: Yes, including for disabled.
Wheelchairs: Excellent access; viewing ramps.
Teas: Own restaurant and coffee shop.
Groups: See this unique working Victorian country pottery, and make your own pot from local clay. Museum of pottery, industrial relics and artefacts. Pre-booked groups preferred.
Transport: None.
Mail order: Yes.
Catalogue: Phone 01768 899123 for catalogue and credit card orders.

We discovered this signpost in Noyon, France, where the first allegiance is clearly to its twin town Hexham.

But is Ham nearby in France, or are travellers being directed to one of the many towns of that name in the UK?

Claremont Garments

2 Doxford Drive, South West Industrial Estate SR8 2RL
(0191) 518 3026

Ladies' wear: lingerie, swimwear, casualwear (bodies, leggings etc), dresses, blouses, skirts, trousers, and tailored suits, coats and jackets. Schoolwear: boys' trousers and shirts; girls' skirts and shirts. Boys' wear: a limited range of casual shirts and trousers.

'All garments are leading chainstore perfects, seconds or ends of lines, and are offered at greatly reduced prices.'

....

In large industrial estate west of the A19.

From A19 exit for 'Peterlee/Horden' B1320. Follow signs to South West Industrial Estate into Shotton Road; at next roundabout (bank on far right corner) go left and next left again. The shop is in second building on left.

Open: Mon–Fri 10–4.30; 10–4. Good Friday.
Closed: All Bank Holidays except Good Friday. Christmas to be arranged, please phone.
Cards: Most major credit cards.
Cars: Own car-park.
Toilets: No; in town centre.
Wheelchairs: Ramp; easy access.
Changing rooms: Yes.
Teas: In town centre.
Groups: Shopping groups welcome, but large groups please phone first.
Transport: Bus to Peterlee town centre.
Mail order: No.

Dewhirst Ltd.

Mill Hill, North West Industrial Estate SR8 5AB
(0191) 586 4525

New purpose-built spacious shop for men's quality suits, sports jackets and blazers, trousers, formal and casual shirts, casual jackets, coats. Ladies' blouses, skirts, trousers, jeans dresses, fashion jackets, blazers, suits, coats. Children's shirts, blouses, skirts, trousers, dresses, jackets, coats, schoolwear.

'Premier factory shop in the Dewhirst Group with the largest display of goods for all the family. Men's quality suits from £80. High quality famous chainstore slight seconds.'

....

In large industrial estate west of the A19.

From A19 exit for 'Peterlee/Horden' B1320. From this exit roundabout follow signs to North West Industrial Estate. The shop is in the first factory on the right.

Open: Mon–Wed 9–5.30; Thur 9–7; Fri 9–6; Sat 9–5; Sun 11–5.
Closed: Easter Sunday; Christmas, Boxing and New Year's Days.
Cards: Access, Connect, Switch, Visa.
Cars: Outside shop.
Toilets: On request.
Wheelchairs: Ramps to huge shop.
Changing rooms: Yes.
Teas: About 1 mile in Peterlee.
Groups: No factory tours; shopping groups welcome, please phone first.
Transport: Buses from Sunderland, Hartlepool, Durham stop outside.
Mail order: No.

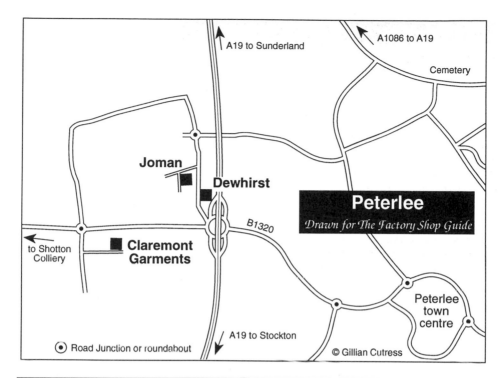

Map labels:
- A19 to Sunderland
- A1086 to A19
- Cemetery
- Joman
- Dewhirst
- B1320
- **Peterlee** — *Drawn for The Factory Shop Guide*
- to Shotton Colliery
- Claremont Garments
- Peterlee town centre
- A19 to Stockton
- ⊙ Road Junction or roundabout
- © Gillian Cutress

Joman Manufacturing Co. Ltd.

1–3 Lister Road, North West Industrial Estate SR8 2RB
(0191) 518 1008

Large stocks of curtain material at factory prices. Specialist manufacturers of curtains, stretch and loose covers. Mail order ends of lines – car seat covers, scatter cushions, underblankets etc; also caravan upholstery covers and curtains.

'Made-to-measure service. Firsts and seconds at factory prices.'

In large industrial estate west of the A19.

From A19 exit for 'Peterlee/Horden' on B1320. From this exit roundabout, follow signs to North West Industrial Estate. Pass Dewhirst on right and take next left (into Lister Road). Joman is in first building on the left.

Open: Mon–Fri 9–5; Sat 10–4.
Closed: Bank Holidays; Christmas–New Year.
Cards: None.
Cars: Outside shop.
Toilets: Yes.
Wheelchairs: Easy access to large shop.
Teas: In town.
Groups: Pre-booked groups of shoppers welcome; please contact Mr Chapman or Mr Hall.
Transport: Sunderland, Hartlepool and Durham buses stop in vicinity.
Mail order: No.

Dewhirst Ltd.

Junction of West Coatham Lane & Limerick Road TS10 5QC
(01642) 472391/2

Men's quality suits, sports jackets and blazers, trousers, formal and casual shirts, casual jackets, coats. Ladies' blouses, skirts, trousers, jeans, dresses, fashion jackets and blazers, suits, casual jackets, coats. Children's shirts, blouses, skirts, trousers, dresses, jackets, coats, schoolwear.

'Products are high quality famous chainstore slight seconds.
Men's quality suits from £80.'

West of Redcar, close to ICI Wilton works and British Steel.

From Middlesbrough or Redcar on the trunk road A1085: at roundabout, turn towards Dormanstown Industrial Estate where signed. Dewhirst is first factory on left (Limerick Road), clearly marked.

From Middlesbrough on A66: go towards Redcar and you come on to A1085. At roundabout, turn towards Dormanstown Industrial Estate where signed. Dewhirst is first factory on left (Limerick Road), clearly marked.

Open: Mon–Fri 9–5.30; Sat 9–5; Sun 10.30–4.30. Bank Holidays.
Closed: Good Friday; Easter Sunday; Christmas, Boxing and New Year's Days.
Cards: Access, Connect, Switch, Visa.
Cars: Own car-park.
Toilets: No.
Wheelchairs: One small step.
Changing rooms: Yes.
Teas: No.
Groups: No factory tours, but groups of shoppers always welcome (prior phone call appreciated).
Transport: Cleveland Transit and United buses operate Redcar–Middlesbrough services via Dormanstown; all stop outside factory.
Mail order: No.

Delcor Furniture

Double Row NE25 0PR
(0191) 237 1303/2395

Large range of upholstered sofas, chairs, sofa beds, bedroom chairs, scatter cushions, fabrics and accessories.

'Sofas from £399.'

North of Seaton Delaval.

From Seaton Delaval: take A192 towards Cramlington. Pass Hastings Arms pub on left, turn right at mini-roundabout into Double Row.*

From A189 southbound: take the A192 to Seaton Delaval. Cross A1061 (roundabout) and after 1.5 miles turn left at mini-roundabout signposted to Hartley.*

From all other directions: go into Seaton Delaval and at roundabout in town centre take A192 to Cramlington. Pass Hastings Arms pub on left, turn right at mini-roundabout into Double Row.*

*Delcor is 400 yds on the left.

Open: Mon–Fri 9–5; Sat 10–4. Bank Holidays: phone for dates and special opening times.
Closed: Christmas, Boxing and New Year's Days.
Cards: None
Cars: Free parking on premises.
Toilets: Facilities available.
Wheelchairs: Three steps to huge shop on ground floor; stairs to first floor.
Tea: Local village cafeteria and pub.
Groups: No.
Transport: Difficult.
Mail order: Yes.
Catalogue: Yes.

58   Sedbergh   Cumbria

Farfield Clothing
Farfield Mill LA10 5LW
(015396) 20169 (fax 015396 21716)

Soft warm quality British polar fleece jackets and jumpers in a paintbox range of colours and styles for all ages. Children's wear from own 'Tough Customer' collection and own 'Original' fibre pile jackets and jerkins.

'A real factory shop selling own brands. Firsts and seconds. At least 25% reduction over the whole range. Example: seconds of polar fleece adult jackets and jumpers £19.99.'

....

About 1 mile south-east of Sedbergh.

From Sedbergh: follow signs to Hawes (A684). This shop, clearly signed, is on the left. Go along the drive to the mill.

From Hawes along the A684: pass the Frostow Methodist Chapel on the left, and the mill is just over 1/2 mile on the right. Go slowly as you have to turn quite sharply into the drive.

Open: Mon–Fri 9–5; Sat 9–1.
Closed: Christmas and New Year.
Cards: Access, Mastercard, Visa.
Cars: In the mill yard.
Toilets: Yes.
Wheelchairs: No steps, easy access.
Changing rooms: No, but welcome to try things on.
Teas: Posthorn or Copper Kettle café in Sedbergh 1 mile away.
Groups: For group visits to mill or shop please book with Mrs Jean Pearson. Maximum 10 persons; no charge.
Transport: Bus Kendal–Sedbergh town; or Settle–Carlisle railway to Garsdale station (6 miles).
Mail order: Yes.
Catalogue: Free brochure. Please telephone. 'Farfield' and 'Tough Customer' clothing available by mail order.

59   Shap   Cumbria

K Shoes
Main Street LA10 3NL
(01931) 716648

Wide choice of shoes, sandals, walking boots, slippers and trainers including a good selection of footwear from *K Shoes, Springers, Clarks, CICA, Dr Martens, Puma* and *Hi-Tec*. Also handbags and luggage.

'Average saving of 30% on normal high street prices for perfect shoes. Discontinued lines and slight sub-standards for men, women and children. Self-select store but trained staff to measure feet and give assistance where needed.'

....

On A6, 12 miles south of Penrith and 18 miles north of Kendal, in centre of Shap.

From M6 exit 39: go right at road junction into village. Well marked shop is on left opposite school.

From Penrith on A6: pass Shell petrol station on left: shop is 400 yds on right.

From Kendal: pass King's Arms Hotel on left: shop is 400 yds on left just past NatWest Bank.

Open: Mon–Sat 9–5; Bank Holidays 10–5.
Closed: Christmas, Boxing and New Year's Days.
Cards: Access, Switch, Visa.
Cars: Outside shop; public car-park across street 80 yds south.
Toilets: In public car-park.
Wheelchairs: Easy access to small shop.
Teas: In Shap.
Groups: Coach parties welcome, concessions for drivers and organisers. £1 voucher per passenger towards purchases.
Transport: Any bus to Shap.
Mail order: No.

60　Shildon　Co. Durham

Durham Clothing Co. Ltd.
Dabble Duck Industrial Estate DL4 2QK
(01388) 777226

Men's suits, jackets and trousers; ladies' jackets, trousers and skirts. Dinner suits, shirts, ties.

'First quality goods at factory prices.'

....

On the south side of Shildon.
　From A1(M): take A68 then A6072, following signs to Shildon. As you approach Shildon, go left at first roundabout, right at second roundabout, and right again at next roundabout.*
　From Bishop Auckland on A6072: cross first roundabout, go left at second roundabout and right at next roundabout.*
　*Take first left on to Dabble Duck Industrial Estate: factory is second on left.

Open: Mon–Thur 10–3; Fri 12–5; Sat 10–4; Bank Holidays 10–4.
Closed: Christmas Day.
Cards: None.
Cars: Own parking.
Toilets: Yes.
Wheelchairs: Stairs to medium sized shop on first floor.
Changing rooms: Yes.
Teas: In Shildon.
Groups: Shopping groups welcome; please telephone first.
Transport: Local buses stop 100 yds away; 5 minutes' walk from station.
Mail order: No.

61　South Shields　Tyne & Wear

Claremont Garments
Rekendyke Ind. Est., Eldon Street NE33 5BT (0191) 454 8822

Ladies' wear: lingerie, swimwear, casualwear (bodies, leggings etc), dresses, blouses, skirts, trousers, and tailored suits, coats and jackets. Schoolwear: boys' trousers and shirts; girls' skirts and shirts. Boys' wear: a limited range of casual shirts and trousers.

'All garments are leading chainstore perfects, seconds or ends of lines, and are offered at greatly reduced prices.'

....

About 1/2 mile south-west of the town centre.
　From South Shields town centre: take any road north towards the river (cranes at the docks); turn left for 'Riverside B1302'. At a roundabout where the A194 branches left you keep following signs to 'Riverside'. Pass large Halfords on left; & the 'Tyne Lodge' pub on the right, follow road round to the left and turn right opposite mosque into Eldon Street. Take second right into West Walpole St.*
　From the Tyne Tunnel south entrance: follow signs to Sth Shields. Go under two railway bridges and turn left where signed to 'Riverside B1302'. Turn left at Tyne Dock public house, then right into South Eldon Street. Continue over next crossing and take first left into West Walpole Street.*
　*Claremont shop is in the third building on the right.

Open: Mon–Fri 9–4.30; Sat 9.30–2.30.
Closed: Most Bank Holidays, please phone to check.
Cards: Most major credit cards.
Cars: Own car-park.
Toilets: In Frederick Street in town.
Wheelchairs: No steps; easy access.
Changing rooms: Yes.
Teas: In Frederick Street in town.
Groups: Shopping groups welcome, but large groups please phone first.
Transport: Chichester Metro station.
Mail order: No.

Black & Decker Service Centre

Green Lane DL16 6JH
(01388) 422429

Full range of *Black & Decker* accessories and reconditioned tools with full warranty. Also servicing of power tools available.

'Reconditioned tools at very reasonable prices. Exchange service available.'

....

On north-east side of Spennymoor.
    From Durham going south on A167(T): go right towards Spennymoor at roundabout on to A688.
    From A688 (Spennymoor town by-pass): turn into Green Lane Industrial Estate (signposted) at roundabout. At next roundabout turn right, following signs.

Open: Mon–Fri 8.30–5 (Wed 9.30–5); Sat 8.30–12.30.
Closed: Bank Holidays. Christmas–New Year.
Cards: Access, Switch, Visa.
Cars: Special visitors' car-park.
Toilets: No.
Wheelchairs: Easy access to shop with large stock.
Teas: In Spennymoor.
Groups: No factory tours. Groups of shoppers always welcome – prior phone call please.
Transport: 15 minutes' walk from town centre.
Mail order: Yes. No restrictions on what sent by mail order.
Catalogue: No.

Famous Fashion Discounts

Chandlers Wharf, Bridge Road TS18 3BA   *(01642) 608205*

Huge selection of top brands including ladies' fashions, men's suits, men's casual wear, children's wear, lingerie, baggage, shoes, gifts and linens. Brands include *Windsmoor, Planet, Gossard, Centaur, Hush Puppies, Lilley & Skinner, Lee Cooper, Dannimac, Farah, Falmer, Joe Bloggs, Fruit of the Loom, Michael de Leon, Accord* and *Coloroll.*

'A bargain-hunter's paradise. Current and end of season ranges, overstocks etc, all at factory prices. Blouses from £12, suits from £75. Large reductions from high street prices.'

....

On south side of town centre, next to Netto.
    From A19 going south: take A1046 at Haverton Hill for Stockton. Turn right at large roundabout with Wickes DIY on left. Continue along Portrack Lane; bear left (Reg Vardy on right). At small roundabout go left towards Thornaby, follow river and turn left at large roundabout (shop on left). Turn left at next lights in front of Thrust petrol into car-park.
    From Darlington or Middlesbrough on A66: exit for A1130 for Stockton centre. At lights turn right, then left at roundabout onto A1045 (one way), straight over mini roundabout. Follow round to lights, go straight at next lights and over Victoria bridge and "SCS" on left. At lights with Thrust petrol on right turn right into car-park.

Open: Mon–Fri 9.30–5.30 (Tues 10–5.30); Sat 9–6; Sun 11–5. Bank Holidays 10–5.
Closed: Christmas Day.
Cards: Access, Joplings Storecard, Visa.
Cars: Large free car-park.
Toilets: Yes (gents up steps).
Wheelchairs: Store on one level, gents' toilet up steps.
Changing rooms: Yes.
Teas: In-store coffee shop; hot and cold drinks and wide range of snacks.
Groups: Shopping groups always welcome but prior phone call to Pat Gibbins (store manager) appreciated. Two coach–parking bays at rear.
Transport: Bus stop outside. Transit bus nos. 37, 52, 54, 58, 63, 64, 75, 80, 84, 181, 113, 114; TMS 37, 116, 598; Tees United bus nos. 235, 268, 269, 272; Express bus nos. X68, X73.
Mail order: No.

Wynsors World of Shoes

Parkfield Road, off Bridge Road TS18 3DJ
(01642) 672525

Men's, ladies' and girls' leather and synthetic fashion shoes, bags and sundries from all over the world, including many famous names.

'Special monthly offers with at least 50% reductions. Major sales in January and July.'

....

On south side of town centre, in new small retail park.
   From A19 going north or south: go on to A66 towards Darlington.*
   From Darlington or Middlesbrough on A66: exit for A135 for Stockton west and Yarm. At end of slip road follow signs to Stockton. At T-junction with lights go right, pass the Lord's Tavern on left; at small roundabout fork right and at second roundabout turn right into Parkfield Road.
   On foot from town: with WH Smith on left, go along Bridge Street. Cross over roundabout into Parkfield Road.*
   ****Take second left into retail estate. Shop first on left.**

Open: Mon–Wed 9–5.30; Thur–Fri 9–8.00; Sat 9–5.30; Sun 10–4. Bank Holidays.
Closed: Christmas, Boxing and New Year's Days.
Cards: Access, Style, Switch, Visa.
Cars: Own large car-park.
Toilets: No.
Wheelchairs: Easy access.
Teas: Lots of places in Stockton High Street.
Groups: Shopping groups welcome. Prior phone call appreciated.
Transport: Any bus or train to Stockton.
Mail order: No.

Dewhirst Ltd.

Pennywell Industrial Estate, Pennywell SR4 9EM
(0191) 534 7928

Men's quality suits, sports jackets and blazers, trousers, shirts, casual jackets, coats. Ladies' blouses, skirts, trousers, dresses, fashion jackets, blazers, suits, casual jackets, coats. Children's shirts, blouses, skirts, trousers, dresses, jackets, coats, schoolwear.

'Products high quality famous chainstore slight seconds. Men's quality suits from £80.'

....

West of Sunderland, just off A19 Sunderland by-pass at junction with A183 (Chester-le-Street road).
   From this junction turn towards Sunderland and into Pennywell Industrial Estate at first roundabout. Take first right and go right again to go around Dewhirst building. Shop is on left, clearly signed.

Open: Mon–Fri 9–5.30; Sat 9–5; Sun 11–5. Bank Holidays.
Closed: Good Friday; Easter Sunday; Christmas, Boxing and New Year's Days.
Cards: Access, Connect, Switch, Visa.
Cars: In factory grounds.
Toilets: No.
Wheelchairs: One step then four steps to large shop.
Changing rooms: Yes.
Teas: No.
Groups: Welcome – please phone first.
Transport: Buses to Sunderland from Consett, Chester-le-Street, Wrighton stop outside shop.
Mail order: No.

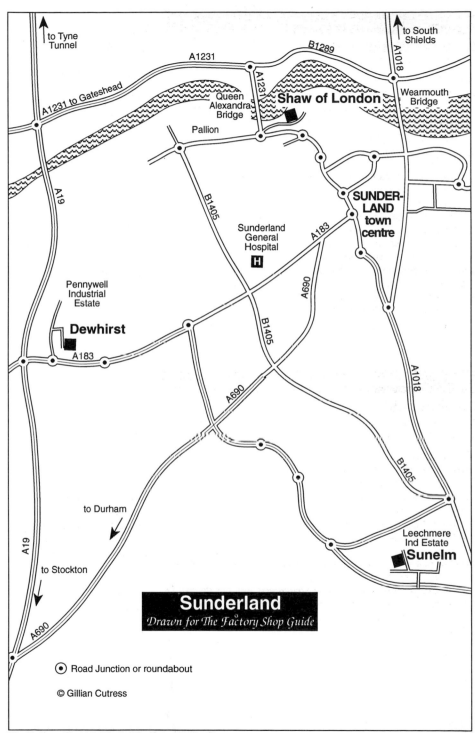

to Tyne Tunnel

to South Shields

A1231

B1289

A1231 to Gateshead

A1231

Queen Alexandra Bridge

Shaw of London

Wearmouth Bridge

A1018

Pallion

A19

B1405

Sunderland General Hospital

H

A183

SUNDER-LAND town centre

Pennywell Industrial Estate

A690

B1405

A1018

Dewhirst

A183

A690

B1405

to Durham

A19

to Stockton

A690

Leechmere Ind Estate

Sunelm

Sunderland
Drawn for The Factory Shop Guide

⊙ Road Junction or roundabout

© Gillian Cutress

Shaw of London (Furniture) Ltd.
Deptford Terrace SR4 6DD
(0191) 564 0666

High quality dining room furniture, lounge suites and occasional furniture in classical and reproduction style in various timbers. Also make up furniture to customers' requirements.

'Perfects at factory prices, ends of lines, prototypes and seconds. Individuals can see their furniture being made.'

Off the A1231 north-west of town centre.
    From town centre: follow signs to Newcastle via A1231. Pass large Ford garage on Trimdon Street. At second roundabout go right following signs to Deptford.*
    From A19: take A1231 to Sunderland following town centre route. Go south over River Wear on large Queen Alexandra Bridge; immediately after the bridge turn left signposted Deptford.*
    ***Factory is 1/2 mile on left, set back in own grounds.**

Open: Mon–Fri 9–5; Sat and Bank Holidays by appointment.
Closed: Please check for Christmas, New Year and Easter openings.
Cards: Access, MasterCard, Visa.
Cars: Own car-park.
Toilets: Ask if required.
Wheelchairs: Unfortunately no access.
Teas: Good quality vending machine on premises for hot and cold drinks.
Groups: Tours by appointment; small shopping groups welcome anytime, larger groups please phone first.
Transport: Difficult.
Mail order: No.

Sunelm Products Sheltered Workshops
Leechmere Industrial Estate SR2 9TO
(0191) 521 1721

Beds and mattresses in all standard sizes. Occasional furniture including coffee tables and nests of tables. Pine bedroom furniture.

'Seconds and ends of lines always available.'

At the back of Asda.
    From A1(M): take A183 or A690 for Sunderland, cross A19(T), turn right at signs for Grangetown. At roundabout with signs to 'Leechmere Industrial Estate EAST' fork right and take next left.*
    From Teeside on A19: turn on to A1018 for Sunderland. Go through to Ryhope and turn left at first roundabout, straight over next roundabout, then first right.*
    From Sunderland centre: take A1018 south. When the dual-carriage section ends, pass Fina petrol station on left and turn right at second roundabout, then first right.*
    ***In industrial estate go first left then first right. Car-park is immediately on left.**

Open: Mon–Thur 9–4; Fri 9–3.
Closed: Bank Holidays; Christmas–New Year.
Cards: No.
Cars: Own car-park.
Toilets: Yes.
Wheelchairs: Easy access.
Teas: In Sunderland.
Groups: Groups please telephone sales office first.
Transport: Buses from Sunderland to Asda.

Heron Glass

Unit 2, The Gill LA12 7BL
(01229) 581121

Irridescent and studio glass, vases, perfume bottles, glass animals, paperweights, lampshades, desk, ceiling, wall lighting and accessories. All hand-made.

'Perfects at considerably below normal high street prices; seconds and special offers.'

North-west of the town centre.
 From the east on A590: turn right at the second roundabout into Brewery Street (one-way). *
 From Barrow on A590 turn left at first roundabout into Brewery Street. *
 ***At mini-roundabout go straight, pass bible shop on left and this shop is about 20 yds on right.**

Open: Mon–Sat 8.30–5 including Bank Holidays.
Closed: Christmas, Boxing and New Year's Days.
Cards: Major credit cards.
Cars: Public car-park across the road.
Toilets: In car-park adjacent.
Wheelchairs: Easy access to small shop.
Teas: In town.
Groups: You can see glass-blowing in progress. Each process shown with pictures and explanation. Free tea and coffee for booked coaches (two days' notice, please).
Transport: BR station 1/2 mile away; regular bus service from Ulverston, but stop nearby.
Mail order: Yes.
Catalogue: Free.

Dainty Supplies Ltd.

Unit 35, Phoenix Road, Crowther Industrial Estate, District 3
NE38 0AA (0191) 416 7886/417 6277

Huge range of craft materials, dress fabrics, ribbons, lace, fur fabric, teddybear noses and components, plastic eyes for soft toys, toy and cushion fillings. Range of decoupage frames and craft frames. Huge selection of miniature items. Frame Craft items. Aida fabric for cross stitch, embroidery silks, tapestry wool, canvas. Bridal fabrics, flowers and accessories. Bridal shoes, veils and sequinned motifs.

'We are a craft person's/sewer's paradise. Garment and toy labelling services. Glad to help with new European Toy Safety Standards.'

On north-west edge of town, near junction of A1(M) and A1.
 From A194(M) south or northbound: exit on to A182 to Washington; go right on to A1231. Take next exit; at round-about go into Crowther Industrial Estate. *
 From A1 Western Bypass southbound: go left on to A1231 for Washington. Go right at first roundabout and turn off at next exit into Crowther Industrial Estate. *
 ***Go to end of Crowther Road, go right and follow road around to left, going uphill. Take next left: Unit 35 is on right.**

Open: Mon–Sat 9–5.
Closed: Bank Holidays; Christmas and Boxing Days.
Cards: Access, Switch, Visa.
Cars: Outside shop.
Toilets: Yes.
Wheelchairs: Easy access.
Teas: In town centre.
Groups: Groups of shoppers and club visits welcome – please phone first.
Transport: Very difficult!
Mail order: Yes.
Catalogue: Free. Write or phone for free price list and samples, mentioning this guide.

S R Leisure

2 Phoenix Road, Crowther Industrial Estate, District 3
NE38 0AD
(0191) 415 3344

Active sportswear. Suppliers to professional skiers, walkers, golfers, fishermen, sailors, canoeists, rowers, rally drivers etc. Large selection of polar fleece, waterproofs, ski wear and accessories from gaiters to Gore-tex boots. Ski clothing hire. Tent/awning repairs and alterations, caravan re-upholstery.

'Corporate leisure wear from baseball caps to waterproofs made to individual requirements. Full embroidery facilities and made-to-measure service.'

On north-west edge of town, near junction of A1(M) and A1.

From A194(M) south or northbound: exit on to A182 to Washington; go right on to A1231. Take next exit; at roundabout go into Crowther Industrial Estate. *

From A1 Western Bypass southbound: go left on to A1231 for Washington. Go right at first roundabout and turn off at next exit into Crowther Industrial Estate. *

***Go to end of Crowther Rd, go right and follow road around to left, going uphill. Phoenix Rd is shortly on right, shop clearly visible.**

Open: Mon–Fri 9–4.45; Sat 9–2.30.
Closed: All Bank Holidays; Christmas–New Year.
Cards: Access, Delta, Eurocard, Mastercard, Switch, Visa.
Cars: Outside shop.
Toilets: No.
Wheelchairs: One step, easy access.
Changing rooms: Yes.
Teas: In town centre.
Groups: Group of shoppers always welcome! Please phone first.
Transport: Very difficult.
Mail order: Yes.
Catalogue: Please phone for price list.

Claremont Garments

Greenfields Industrial Estate, Tindale Crescent DL14 9TR
(01388) 661703

Ladies' wear: lingerie, swimwear, casualwear (bodies, leggings etc), dresses, blouses, skirts, trousers, and tailored suits, coats and jackets. Schoolwear: boys' trousers and shirts; girls' skirts and shirts. Boys' wear: a limited range of casual shirts and trousers.

'All garments are leading chainstore perfects, seconds or ends of lines, and are offered at greatly reduced prices.'

North-east of West Auckland and south-west of Bishop Auckland but these two towns are hard to differentiate! Just off A688 almost opposite Tindale Crescent Hospital.

From Bishop Auckland on A688 (towards West Auckland/ Barnard Castle): go right at traffic lights (signs to Tindale Crescent Hospital). *

From centre of West Auckland: take A688 for Bishop Auckland. At traffic lights with signs to Tindale Crescent Hospital go left. *

From A1(M)/Darlington: turn on to A68; at next roundabout take A6072. Follow signs to West Auckland. Go straight at lights. *

***Industrial estate is 200 yds on left; shop is first on left.**

Open: Mon–Fri 10–4.30; Sat 10–4. Good Friday.
Closed: Bank Holidays (except Good Friday); Christmas and New Year please check.
Cards: Most major cards.
Cars: Own car-park.
Toilets: In Bishop Auckland, 1 mile.
Wheelchairs: One small step to large shop.
Changing rooms: Yes.
Teas: In Morrison's supermarket.
Groups: Shopping groups welcome, but large groups please phone first.
Transport: Buses to Evenwood from Bishop Auckland bus station; stop at Tindale Crescent (traffic lights).
Mail order: No.

Decoflora

Unit 6c, Buddle Road, Clay Flatts CA14 3AY
(01900) 872046

Floral arrangements created in own workshops – dried, silk and artificial flowers. Always large selection of made-up arrangements and raw materials to make your own.

'Cash & carry; have large stock of baskets, brassware and floral sundries at competitive prices.'

....

In industrial estate north of the town.

From Maryport: follow signs to Clay Flatts and industrial estates. Pass the railway station on left and the gasometer on right. Go over roundabout and take first left; shop is around the corner on right.

Froom Whitehaven on A595 and Cockermouth on A66: follow signs to town centre, then 'Town centre, docks, industrial estate', finally to station. At the station turn left, pass the gasometer on left, go straight and roundabout then take first left; shop is around the corner on right.

Open: Mon–Fri 9.30–5 (Wed late night to 6.30); Sat 10–4.
Closed: Bank Holidays; Christmas–New Year.
Cards: Major credit cards, Delta, Switch.
Cars: Outside shop.
Toilets: No.
Wheelchairs: One tiny step.
Teas: Café around the corner.
Groups: No tours.

Linden Upholstery

Unit 11, Clay Flatts CA14 2TQ
(01900) 64787

Upholstered furniture including sofa-beds and three-piece suites made here. Extensive range of fabric designs and colours. Manufactured in any combination or grouping from own designs.

'Quality upholstery, custom built in the fabric of your choice at competitive prices. All perfects. January sales – please check for dates.'

....

In industrial estate a short distance south of the town/station.

From Maryport go south: as you reach Workington, follow signs to Clay Flatts and industrial estates. Pass the railway station on right and the gasometer on left. Go over roundabout then take first right. Shop is 70 yds on right.

From Whitehaven going north on A595 and Cockermouth on A66: follow signs to town centre, then 'Town centre, docks and industrial estate', finally to station. In front of the station turn left, pass the gasometer on left, go straight at the roundabout then take first right. Shop is 70 yds on right.

Open: Mon–Sat 9–5 including Bank Holidays.
Closed: Christmas Eve, Christmas, Boxing and New Year's Days.
Cards: Access, Visa.
Cars: In front of factory.
Toilets: Available if required including for disabled.
Wheelchairs: No steps; reasonable access within showroom.
Teas: In Safeway nearby.
Groups: Shopping groups welcome, but please phone first.
Transport: Local buses five minutes' walk.
Mail order: No.

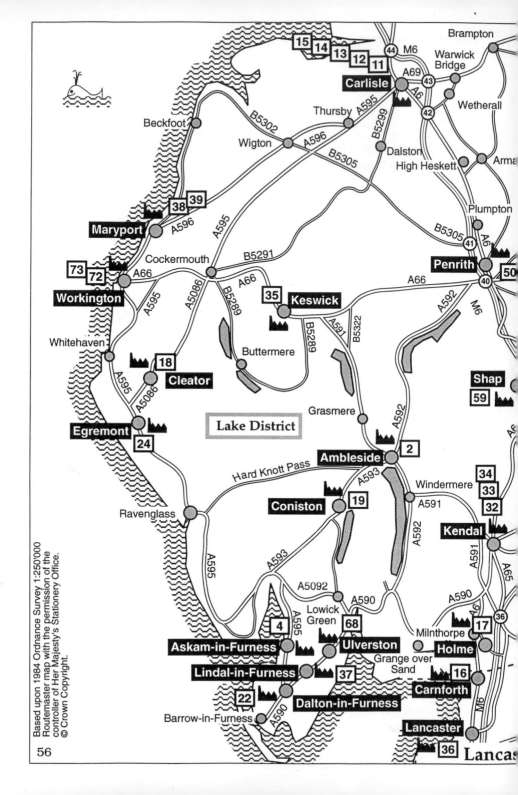

Brampton

15 14 13 12 11 44 M6 Warwick
Bridge

Carlisle A69
43

Thursby A595 42 Wetherall

Beckfoot B5302 B5299

Wigton A596 Dalston Arma
High Heskett

B5305

Plumpton

38 39
A596 B5305 A6

Maryport A595 41

Penrith 50

Cockermouth B5291 A66 40

73 72 A66 A66

Workington A595 A5086 B5289 35 Keswick

Whitehaven A595 B5289 A591 B5322

18 Buttermere A592

Cleator

A5086 Grasmere Shap

Egremont Lake District 59

24 A592

Hard Knott Pass Ambleside 2

Windermere 34
33
32

Coniston 19 A591

Ravenglass A593 A592 Kendal

A595 A5092 A591 A65

Lowick A590
Green A590 A6

A593 4 A595 68 Milnthorpe 17 36

Askam-in-Furness Ulverston Holme

Grange over
Sand

Lindal-in-Furness 37 16

22 Dalton-in-Furness Carnforth

Barrow-in-Furness A590 Lancaster

36 Lanca

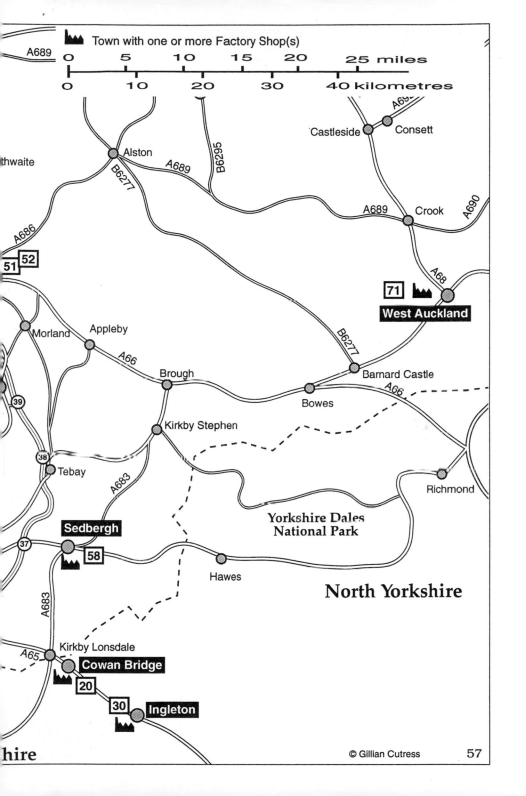

Town with one or more Factory Shop(s)

0   5   10   15   20   25 miles
0   10   20   30   40 kilometres

A689

thwaite

Alston

B6277

A689

B6295

Castleside

Consett

A689

Crook

A690

A686

51 52

A68

71 West Auckland

Morland

Appleby

A66

Brough

B6277

Barnard Castle

A66

Bowes

39

Kirkby Stephen

38

Tebay

A683

Richmond

Sedbergh

58

Yorkshire Dales
National Park

37

Hawes

North Yorkshire

A683

Kirkby Lonsdale

A65

Cowan Bridge

20

30 Ingleton

hire

© Gillian Cutress   57

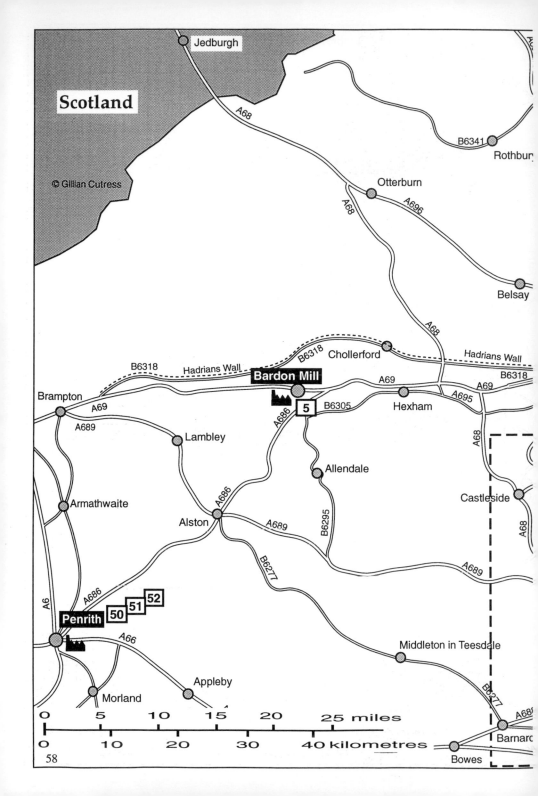

Scotland

© Gillian Cutress

Jedburgh

A68

B6341

Rothbury

Otterburn

A68

A696

A68

Belsay

B6318

Hadrians Wall

B6318

Chollerford

Hadrians Wall

Brampton

B6318

Hadrians Wall

Bardon Mill

A69

A69

B6318

A69

5

B6305

Hexham

A695

A689

Lambley

A686

A68

Allendale

Armathwaite

A686

B6295

Castleside

A68

Alston

A689

A689

B6277

A686

52

51

50

Penrith

A6

A686

A66

Middleton in Teesdale

B6277

Appleby

A686

Morland

Barnard

Bowes

0	5	10	15	20	25 miles

0	10	20	30	40 kilometres

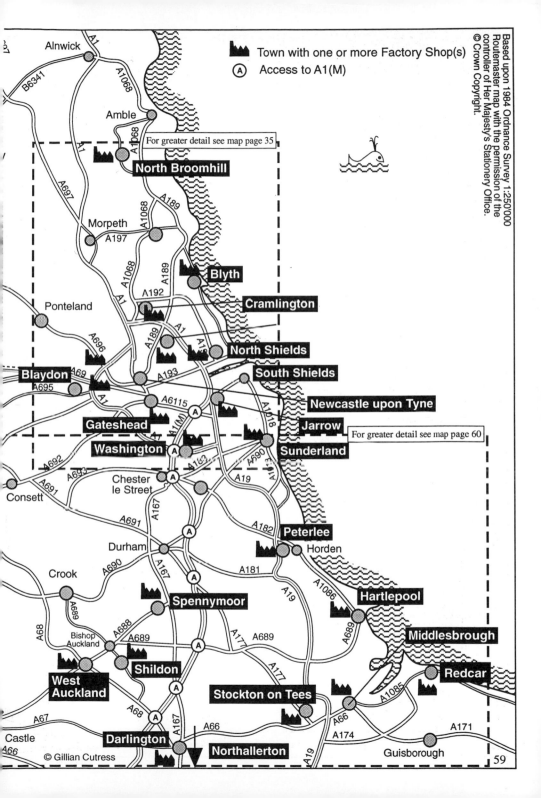

Town with one or more Factory Shop(s)

Ⓐ **Access to A1(M)**

Alnwick

Amble

For greater detail see map page 35

North Broomhill

Morpeth

Blyth

Cramlington

Ponteland

North Shields

Blaydon

South Shields

Newcastle upon Tyne

Gateshead

Jarrow

Washington

Sunderland

For greater detail see map page 60

Consett

Chester le Street

Peterlee

Horden

Durham

Crook

Hartlepool

Spennymoor

Bishop Auckland

Middlesbrough

Shildon

Redcar

West Auckland

Stockton on Tees

Castle

Darlington

Northallerton

Guisborough

© Gillian Cutress

59

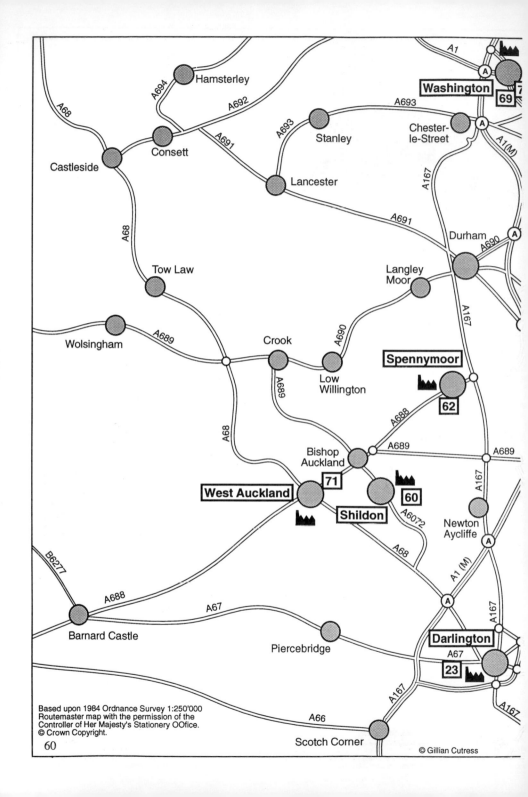

© Gillian Cutress

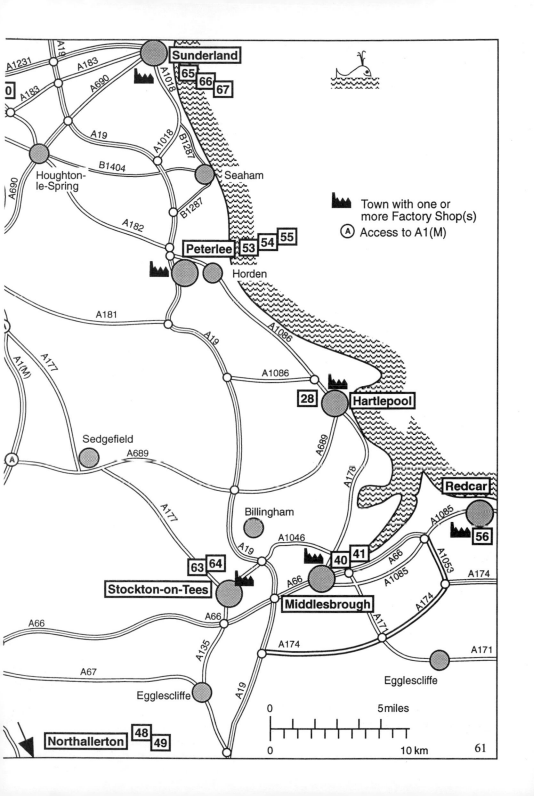

A1231

A183

A690

A183

A19

A1018

Sunderland 65 66 67

Houghton-le-Spring

A690

B1404

A1018

B1287

A19

A182

B1287

Seaham

Town with one or more Factory Shop(s)

Ⓐ Access to A1(M)

Peterlee 53 54 55

Horden

A181

A19

A1086

A1086

28 Hartlepool

A1(M)

A177

Sedgefield

A689

Ⓐ

A177

A19

A689

A178

Billingham

A1046

Redcar

A1085

56

40 41

A66

A1085

A1053

A174

63 64

Stockton-on-Tees

A19

A66

Middlesbrough

A66

A174

A171

A174

A66

A135

A171

Egglescliffe

A67

Egglescliffe

A19

0   5 miles

0   10 km

Which shops do you recommend?

One of the most enjoyable yet totally unexpected aspects of producing these guides is the large number of letters we receive from readers. Some letters recount funny shopping experiences; many provide wonderful information about shops which we ourselves have not yet caught up with; others ask us for specific details.

A recurring request is that we indicate the quality of items sold in the shops. We personally feel unable to provide such information because our opinion would be too subjective. We also know, from the questionnaires which many people are kind enough to return, that views on any one shop vary according to what the customer is looking for. If you require cheap clothing for an economical family beach holiday in Spain, you will be looking for something different from that needed for a luxury cruise in the Cayman Islands. You can obtain both ranges of clothing when you buy direct from the maker and both can be excellent value for money – but how you judge the shop will depend on whether it stocked what you were looking for on the day you went and whether the service was what you expected.

However, in the best traditions of other guide books, we welcome the chance to continue building up information about those shops which you, the shopper, consider offer top value for money, good service, wide ranges of goods – or the reverse! Shopping is much more than just a question of spending money. It is a pleasure – an enjoyable aspect of a day's outing – an essential feature of a holiday. (Would you believe that 50% of money spent on holiday goes on shopping?) When you buy items from shops like the ones described in these books, there is also the 'fun of the chase'.

Wth your help we would like to build up a list of the best factory and mill shops. Please complete the form opposite. Unless you request otherwise, we might use your name in connection with a good report.

We need to know:

the name and address of the shop you visited;
when you shopped there;
what you bought;
the amount you spent;
and how you considered the following aspects:
How welcoming were the staff?
Was the service good/bad/unmemorable?
What did you think of the products for sale?
Did you consider the items represented good value for money?
What was especially good or bad about your shopping trip?

To: Gill Cutress, The Factory Shop Guide, FREEPOST (SW 8510), London SW2 4BR

I should like to comment on the following shop

Name and address of the shop visited ....

....

....

Date of visit .... How much you spent ....

What you bought ....

Comments, anecdotes etc on the shop, service, parking, goods for sale – or whatever attracted your attention!

Where did you buy your guide?..

Your name ....

Your address ....

....

Post code ....

Phone number .... Date ....

If you would like more copies of this form, please give us a ring and we'll post them.
Phone (0181) 678 0593 Fax (0181) 674 1594

To: Gill Cutress, The Factory Shop Guide, FREEPOST (SW 8510), London SW2 4BR

I should like to comment on the following shop

Name and address of the shop visited ....

....

....

Date of visit .... How much you spent ....

What you bought ....

Comments, anecdotes etc on the shop, service, parking, goods for sale – or whatever attracted your attention!

Where did you buy your guide?...

Your name ....

Your address ....

....

Post code ....

Phone number .... Date ....

If you would like more copies of this form, please give us a ring and we'll post them.
Phone (0181) 678 0593 Fax (0181) 674 1594

Would you like a free book next year?

More manufacturers are opening factory shops. If you have enjoyed visiting other shops, either here, or in France or elsewhere in the world, we should be delighted to hear about them. If you are the first person to send us new details which are published next year, we shall be happy to send you a free copy of the new guide.

Name of company ....
Address ....
What do they sell? ....

Name of company ....
Address ....
What do they sell? ....

Name of company ....
Address ....
What do they sell? ....

Name of company ....
Address ....
What do they sell? ....

Where did you buy your copy of this guide? ....
How did you hear about it? ....

Your name ....
Your address ....
....
Town..
Post code..
Your phone no...
Date ....

Readers in Britain only, please send to:
Factory Shop Guide, FREEPOST (SW 8510) London SW2 4BR
(0181) 678 0593   fax (0181) 674 0594

How can we make this guide even more useful?

To help us give you the information you are looking for, please fill in this questionnaire.

SPECIAL OFFER – SAVE 60p ON YOUR NEXT ORDER! *Send (no stamp needed) this fully completed form back to us and we will send you a 60p voucher to use when you next order any of our titles from us.*

Why do you like Factory Shopping?

Is there anything you don't like about Factory Shops?

Which shops do you prefer? (please tick only one answer)
a. Shops which sell only those goods which they make themselves
b. Shops with a mixture of items, including related bought-in goods
c. Shops which sell anything, including imported items, if they are cheap
d. No preferences
e. Factory outlet centres
Any other comments?

How much did you spend at the last Factory Shop you visited?
a. Less than £10
b. £10 or over but under £15
c. £15 or over but under £20
d. £20 and over
e. £30 and over
f. £100 and over
g. £200 and over

Which items in Factory Shops interest you in particular?
a. Knitting wools
b. Sewing materials
c. Craft materials
d. Pottery & porcelain
e. Glassware
f. Children's clothing
g. Household linens, furnishings
h. General clothing
i. Designer clothing
j. Carpets
k. Furniture
l. What else?

Have you visited Factory Shops
a. While on holiday?   Often / Sometimes / Not at all
b. While travelling on business?   Often / Sometimes / Not at all
c. When visiting relatives?   Often / Sometimes / Not at all
d. During day trips from home?   Often / Sometimes / Not at all

Have you visited any of the 'factory outlet centres'?   Yes / Not yet
If yes, which one(s)?

On the day you last went to a Factory Shop, how many individual Factory Shops did you visit in total?

Provided you have time, do you enjoy touring the factory itself when you visit a Factory Shop?
Very much / it's OK / not much / no thanks
What is the furthest you have travelled especially to go to a particular Factory Shop?

Did you buy your own copy of this Guide? Yes / No   **Was the book a present?** Yes / No
Have you given a copy to anyone else?   Yes / No
Have you previously bought other Factory Shop Guides? Yes / No   If yes, which?

How many of the shops, mentioned in this book, were new to you? Just a few / Quite a lot / Almost all
How many people have looked through your copy of this Guide? (include yourself!)
Are you male / female?
Which age bracket are you in?   Under 20 20–29 30–39 40–49 50–59 60–69 70+
Which newspaper(s) do you read?   Sun Mail Express Telegraph Times Independent Guardian
                                       Mirror Observer Sunday Times Others
Which weekly and monthly magazines do you see regularly?

What other information would you like this guide to give?

Any other comments?

Please send the following books to me:

.....copy(ies) of the **Derbys/Notts/Lincs Guide** at £4.50 each   £   .

.....copy(ies) of the **Staffordshire & the Potteries Guide** at £3.95 each   £   .

.....copy(ies) of the **Yorks/Humberside Guide** at £3.95 each   £   .

.....copy(ies) of the **Northern England Guide** at £3.95 each   £   .

.....copy(ies) of the **Leics/Northants/Bedford Guide** at £3.95 each   £   .

.....copy(ies) of the **Western Midlands Guide** at £3.95 each   £   .

.....copy(ies) of the **North-West England/North Wales Guide** £4.50   £   .

.....copy(ies) of the **Scotland Guide** at £4.50 each   £   .

.....copy(ies) of the **E Anglia & SE England Guide** at £4.50 each   £   .

.....copy(ies) of the **SW England & S Wales Guide** at £4.50 each   £   .

P&p within UK: 60p each above book, max £3.50   £   .

.....copy(ies) of the **Great British Factory Shop Guide** at £14.95 each   £   .

.....copy(ies) of the **Italian Guide** at £12.95 each   £   .

.....copy(ies) of the **Northern France Guide** at £9.95 each   £   .

.....copy(ies) of the **Sweden Guide** at £8.95 each   £   .

.....copy(ies) **Gardeners' Atlas (Notts/Derbys/S Yorks)** at £6.95   £   .

.....copy(ies) **Gardeners' Atlas (Surrey, Sussex, Middx)** at £6.95   £   .

P&p within UK: £1 each above book, max £3.50   £   .

I enclose a cheque *or* **please debit my Access / MasterCard / Visa**
Cheques made payable to G. Cutress   **GRAND TOTAL**   £   .

Credit card Access / MasterCard / Visa

No. .... **Expiry date** ....

Name .... **Tel. no.** ....

Address ....

....

Town .... **Post code** ....

Signed .... **Date** ....

Readers in Britain only, please send to: The Factory Shop Guide,
FREEPOST (SW 8510) London SW2 4BR   Phone (0181) 678 0593   Fax (0181) 674 1594

Overseas readers, please send your credit card details to:
The Factory Shop Guide, 1 Rosebery Mews, Rosebery Road, London SW2 4DQ
for airmail delivery (actual postage plus small packing fee).

**SPECIAL MESSAGE TO READERS WHO HAVE PREVIOUSLY SENT US THE FULLY
COMPLETED FORM ON p. 66: DON'T FORGET TO ENCLOSE
YOUR 60p 'THANK YOU' VOUCHER!**

I would like to send a gift to the following person:

Name..

Address ....

Town.. Post Code ....

.....copy (ies) of the **Derbys/Notts/Lincs Guide** at £4.50 each   £   .

.....copy (ies) of the **Staffordshire & the Potteries Guide** at £3.95 each   £   .

.....copy (ies) of the **Yorks/Humberside Guide** at £3.95 each   £   .

.....copy (ies) of the **Northern England Guide** at £3.95 each   £   .

.....copy (ies) of the **Leics/Northants/Bedford Guide** at £3.95 each   £   .

.....copy (ies) of the **Western Midlands Guide** at £3.95 each   £   .

.....copy (ies) of the **North-West England/North Wales Guide** £4.50   £   .

.....copy (ies) of the **Scotland Guide** at £4.50 each   £   .

.....copy (ies) of the **E Anglia & SE England Guide** at £4.50 each   £   .

.....copy (ies) of the **SW England & S Wales Guide** at £4.50 each   £   .

P&p within UK: 60p each above book, max £3.50   £   .

.....copy (ies) of the **Great British Factory Shop Guide** at £14.95 each   £   .

.....copy (ies) of the **Italian Guide** at £12.95 each   £   .

.....copy (ies) of the **Northern France Guide** at £9.95 each   £   .

.....copy (ies) of the **Sweden Guide** at £8.95 each   £   .

.....copy (ies) **Gardeners' Atlas (Notts/Derbys/S Yorks)** at £6.95   £   .

.....copy (ies) **Gardeners' Atlas (Surrey, Sussex, Middx)** at £6.95   £   .

P&p within UK: £1 each above book, max £3.50   £   .

I enclose a cheque *or* please debit my Access / MasterCard / Visa
Cheques made payable to G. Cutress   **GRAND TOTAL**   £   .

Credit card Access / MasterCard / Visa

No. .... Expiry date ....

Your name .... Tel. no. ....

Your address ....

....

Town .... Post code ....

Signed .... Date ....

Readers in Britain only, please send to: The Factory Shop Guide,
FREEPOST (SW 8510) London SW2 4BR Phone (0181) 678 0593 Fax (0181) 674 1594

Overseas readers, please send your credit card details to:
The Factory Shop Guide, 1 Rosebery Mews, Rosebery Road, London SW2 4DQ
for airmail delivery (actual postage plus small packing fee).

The *Official* Great British Factory Shop Guide

The second edition of this guide, with dozens of new shops and totally updated, is essential for every shrewd shopper. It not only gives the why, what, how and where of factory shopping, but also contains over 500 pages and full page maps with a mass of vital information on nearly 800 factory shops. We believe this book is especially useful for visitors and people who tour the UK on business or pleasure, or who are seeking specific items. This guide complements our very successful regional books as it is arranged by product, with nineteen chapters on clothing, footwear, carpets, garden items, glass and cutlery, electrical appliances, pottery, accessories, food and drink etc. It also gives full details about the new factory shop villages. The shops cover the entire spectrum of items to buy, from top of the market evening wear to serviceable socks for children, from designer bags which are displayed in leading international department stores to plastic holdalls for taking sandwiches to the football match. Details about which companies offer mail order are included. This book has especially drawn maps, detailed indexes of products sold, and lists of companies with factory shops, and shops by county. There are lots of cross-references.

Scotland

From the Islands and John O'Groats to Hadrian's Wall: about 100 enticing shops for superb cashmere knitwear and international designer woven cashmere; wools and co-ordinated knitwear; tartans and kilts. Taste and buy top quality Scottish jams & soups, shortbread & biscuits, and find out which whisky distilleries are open to visitors. Several super potteries for cookware and animal figurines, decorative boxes, cut and engraved crystal glassware, coloured glass paperweights, curtaining; shiny fashion raincoats, designer sweatshirts, brand name jeans, well known brands of ladies' skirts, jackets, coats, workwear, beds, bedding, garden furniture, terracotta pots, giant casseroles, household linens, sheeting, silk scarves, bodywarmers, lightweight raincoats, sheepskin jackets, stylish children's leisurewear and family clothing. From the Shetlands and Hebrides to Wick, Lochinver, Ullapool, Oban, Inverness, Aberdeen, Perth, Kinross, Dundee, Alva, Stirling, Dunfermline, Bo'ness, Edinburgh, Glasgow area, Dunoon, Kilmarnock, Campbeltown, Ayr, Galashiels, Selkirk and Hawick.

Other Factory Shop Guides in the series

Ten regional guides show you how to find top value for money in mill and factory shops in specific areas of the country. Set out in alphabetical order by town, these books contain many detailed street maps together with background information on the regions. These regional guides are ideal for shoppers who wish to discover the factory shops in their own vicinity and for people who are going on holiday to a specific region. They make good presents for people living there too!

Guides are available in good bookshops, WH Smith, Waterstone's, James Thin etc and by mail directly from us.

If you would like to have up-to-date details about current books, please send an SAE or give us a ring for a free leaflet.

Ninety-eight shops for carpets, towels, blouses, children's and family clothing, furnishing fabrics, sofa beds, skiwear, high quality knitwear, co-ordinated home furnishings, lightweight fleece outdoor clothing, garden furniture, knitting yarns (mail order too) and sports wear. Humberside has trousers, jackets, chainstore clothing, table lamps, pottery, footwear, leather and sheepskin coats in Bridlington, Driffield, Hull, Immingham, Scunthorpe, Grimsby (for fresh and smoked fish and Danish specialities). Yorkshire for furnishing fabrics, wallpapers, underwear, shoes, hand-made sprung beds, country furniture, left-handed scissors, cutlery, silverware, glassware, woollen & worsted fabrics, woollen clothing, tapestry kits, craft materials, tablecloths, hats, gloves, dress and curtain velvets. Three factory shop centres. Whitby, York, Ripon, Harrogate, Addingham, Keighley, Skipton, Leeds, Bradford area, Hebden Bridge, Halifax, Holmfirth, Huddersfield, Sheffield, Rotherham, Doncaster.

Nearly 120 shops sell great value spectacles, high performance waterproof clothing, famous name high street fashion garments, outstanding selections of curtain fabrics, every possible style in blinds, unusually wide shoes for people who have difficulty in finding comfortable footwear, useful items for the disabled, all styles of lighting, carpets galore, Christmas cards and wrapping paper, Welsh quarry tiles and caviar spoons. An extraordinary area for bedding, curtain and furnishing fabrics and tiles, including famous brand names. Many make curtains at reasonable cost. Also a wide range of family clothing, rucksacks, sleeping bags, bedding, knitwear, pond liners, garden equipment, lampshades and bases, small electrical items, toys and sewing threads. From Lancaster, Blackpool, Runcorn, Wrexham and Liverpool south to Glossop, including the entire Manchester area.

The ONLY publication with comprehensive details that tells you how to find the world-famous potteries – plus some small ones which you have probably not come across before, including a company making traditional Staffordshire dogs. If you wish to go round the potteries, to watch china made and decorated, or simply want to find excellent value for money, this book tells you where, when and how. Staffordshire companies make much more than china! This book lets you into the secrets of other companies, some with equally famous names, for exquisite enamelled boxes, clothing, wax jackets, hand-cut crystal, countrywear, shoes, lingerie and knitwear. Wilmslow, Leek, Biddulph, Stafford, Rugeley, Tutbury, Burton & Tamworth. 39 potteries in Stoke. Specially drawn maps of individual towns. Information for overseas visitors on how to get china home.

Nowhere else will you find such detailed information, along with specially drawn maps, of the traditional hand-cut full lead crystal companies in the Stourbridge area, west of Birmingham. Also for the fascinating Jewellery Quarter in Birmingham offering hand-crafted individual jewellery at excellent prices, and skilled repairs. One of the best areas for superb selections of carpets, natural fibre floor coverings, curtains, children's outdoor toys, leather shoes, vibrant hand painted scarves and ties, ladies' clothing, trousers, pottery, tableware (Royal Worcester), hair dryers, small electrical items, Christmas tree lights, fitted kitchens, silver plated cutlery and trays etc, brass and copper items, house nameplates, all styles in hats and headwear, designer T-shirts, top branded knitwear, leather items, garden pots, lamp-shades and lights. Craven Arms, Telford, Shrewsbury, Stourbridge, Stourport, Walsall, Ross-on-Wye, Kidderminster, Wolverhampton, Birmingham, Tewkesbury, Worcester, Stratford.

Western Midlands

What an amazing area for factory shops! Enticing shops sell knitwear, lingerie, shoes, underwear, lighting, leisurewear, curtains, pottery, earthenware tableware, glassware, terracotta, garden pots, tableware, lace, bridal fabrics, cutlery and an unbelievable range of products previously available from catalogue companies by post. Shops in Lincolnshire for family clothing, excellent knitwear, net curtains, and hand-made sandals. Buy made-to-measure large sized leisurewear, vast variety of clothing for all the family and all activities, including fishing and golfing; baby and chainstore children's wear, luggage, bath cubes and soaps, sweets, silks, marvellous selections of dress fabrics, cooking and kitchenware, curtains and curtaining, decanters, fashion shoes, sports shoes and trainers, cane and a very broad range of upholstered and leather furniture, a huge range of knitwear, hosiery, leather jackets, light fittings, men's suits, jackets and trousers, paperweights, pillows, shirts, stocking fillers, toys, tablecloths, towels, wallcoverings, Welsh dressers and wrapping paper! About 100 shops from Sheffield south to Shepshed.

Derbyshire, Nottinghamshire & Lincolnshire

For shops selling curtains, women's knitwear, sewing machines and spare parts, furnishing fabrics, furniture, walking boots, and garden urns, columns and statues. You can buy super value lighting, lampshades, soaps and shampoos, family shoes and men's leather footwear, Doc Marten's boots, ladies' and family clothing. Also boys' underwear, football boots and a terrific selection of sports clothing, schoolwear, knitting yarns, dress and curtain fabrics, 100% wool sweaters, carpets, bermuda shorts, men's suits, ladies' jackets, safety footwear, socks and Stilton

Leicestershire, Northamptonshire & Bedford

cheese. Also cosmetics, soaps, toiletries, kitchen and home accessories, oven-to-tableware, bedding, handbags, leather goods, curtains, lamp shades, luggage, tablemats, tables, chairs. Ashby, Moira, Shepshed, Coalville, Loughborough, Leicester, Sileby, Wigston, Hinckley, Nuneaton, Oakham; Kettering, Northampton, Wellingborough, Earls Barton; Bedford (for furnishing fabrics) and many other places.

South-West England & South Wales

From Oxfordshire south and west: offering basketware, bedding, family clothing, carpets, floor and wall tiles, famous cider, garden pots and lots of sheepskin products. Kitchenware, fitted kitchens, designer silk wear, some fabrics, lots of footwear (incl. made-to-measure), safety clothing, furniture, crystal glass, handmade paper, knitwear, lamp bases & shades, model animals and houses, a great range of pottery, ribbons, rugs, soft and wooden toys, schoolwear, wools and yarns. From the Channel Islands, thro' Cornwall & Devon to Gloucestershire (tablemats, carpets, tiles) and Oxfordshire (carpets, pottery, furnishing fabrics); Christchurch and Poole; Wiltshire (carpets, underwear, table mats, tiles, ladies' clothing); many shops in Somerset (Clarks Village), Bristol; 29 shops in South Wales for superb cashmere, cut glass, traditional woollen fabrics, cakes, body warmers, boiled sweets, diabetic chocolate, household textiles, ladies' quality clothing.

East Anglia & South-East England

Manufacturers and shoppers are catching on fast in southern England. This edition features 103 shops from Norfolk (sweets, country knitwear, shoes, handbags, famous brand clothing); Suffolk (terracotta kitchen jars, silk, pottery, basketware, leather coats); Cambridgeshire (top quality leather cases and briefcases, famous ladies' wear, mail-order returns); Essex (quality furniture and repairs, dried flowers, jeans, chainstore ends of lines); the Home Counties north of London (world-famous ladies' clothing, designer wear, furnishing fabrics, lingerie, carpets, glass); Bedfordshire (curtaining and furnishing fabrics); London (candles, tableware, stylish shoes, sofa beds, original clock designs, lighting, teak furniture, furnishing fabrics, model kits); Kent (garden pots and furniture, silk ties, shoes, dried flowers); Sussex (lingerie, pots, sewing/knitting supplies, fashion jewellery, trugs, tiles, designer wear); Surrey (cashmere, knitwear, furniture); Hampshire (electric toasters, stainless steel tableware, sportswear, carpets); the Isle of Wight (pottery and glass). Also fish smokeries and an enormous selection of other items!

Northern France

Cross the Channel and discover a little known shopping trail, or 'How to make the most of enticing French products at less than traditional French prices!'. Our innovative and information-packed guide (in English and French) is the first of its kind, ideal for day-trippers and weekenders travelling to France, along with serious Francophiles who have more time in which to seek out the great array of factory shops. Expect to pay about a third less than normal French prices. From Calais and Boulogne east to St Omer and Lille, into Belgium, then south to Cambrai, Laon, Reims, St Quentin and Troyes, the major factory shopping town in France. Enjoy all those tempting French items with that certain French je ne sais quoi – such as outstanding ranges of co-ordinated household linens by leading international names; *Le Creuset* ovenware (seconds can cost as little as a third of the normal UK retail price!); *Cristal d'Arques* tableware; sumptuous *YSL, Daniel Hechter, Descamps, Primrose Bordier* and *Olivier Desforges* designer name bathrobes; exquisite lacy lingerie; *Le Bourget, DD* and *Zanzi* hosiery; stylish women's wear (including *Weill of Paris* and *Paul Mausner*); *Levi's* and *Wrangler* leisurewear; *Le Coq Sportif* and *Adidas* sportswear; *Bally* shoes; ski clothing; hand-made chocolate; traditional French pottery including snail plates!; children's clothes, including *Petit Bateau, Catimini* and *Osh Kosh*; and outstanding men's jackets and suits. With 234 shops, including four interesting factory outlet centres, this guide gives detailed directions to and a photo of each shop. The price guide indicates what you can expect to pay. Champagne trails near Rheims add fizz to your shopping!

Bargain Hunting in Italy

This personally researched book is by a shopping fiend living in Milan. 'Italy produces and exports many beautiful luxury goods, be it silks, shoes, furniture or household wares', so she has explored the world of seconds, close-outs, showroom models, samples, ends of lines, bargain basements and secondhand shops. In English and Italian, this 320-page guide details 600 places set out by province (38 shops around Como, 33 in Florence area, seven near Perugia, 41 entries for Rome, 5 for Bologna, 5 for Verona, 134 in Milan etc). This 'extremely useful guide for the intelligent consumer in search of expensive goods at less expensive prices ...' is available in the UK only from *The Factory Shop Guide*.

South Africa

There are 300 factory shops in the Cape Town area. If you are going there on holiday, take advantage of the low Rand. You can find good buys in men's clothing and explore a wide variety of shops selling women's clothing, shoes, sportswear etc. If searching out the shops by yourself seems too daunting, you can join a tour and be guided round the shops by expert shopper Pam Black. For a free leaflet about Pam's books *The A—Z of Factory Shops* for the Cape area or Natal please send us an SAE. By credit card, you can arrange for a book to be sent to yourself or directly to friends in South Africa.

Sweden

We have discovered a book which tells you how to save money at Swedish factory shops! With world-famous names in glass, such as *Boda, Orrefors* and *Kosta Boda*, and in household articles, such as *Dorre* and *Scandia* – all of which offer items at 30–50% below normal retail prices – this book should soon cover its cost even if you use it just a few times on your Swedish holiday. For people who admire Swedish design but who are reluctant to pay traditional Swedish prices. Available in the UK only from *The Factory Shop Guide*.

Companies with Factory Shops

NUMBERS refer to the ENTRIES, NOT the PAGES

Abbey Horn of Lakeland	17	Carnforth (Holme)
Barbour	31	Jarrow
Bargain Baggage Factory Shop	46	North Shields
Barker Shoes	35	Keswick
Black & Decker Service Centre	62	Spennymoor
Briggs & Shoe Mines	2	Ambleside
Briggs & Shoe Mines	11	Carlisle
Briggs & Shoe Mines	32	Kendal
Briggs & Shoe Mines	50	Penrith
Burberrys	9	Blyth
Calvert's Carpets	48	Northallerton
Catalogue Bargain Shop	40	Middlesbrough
Catalogue Bargain Shop	43	Newcastle upon Tyne
CB Home Furnishings	49	Northallerton
Claremont Garments	10	Blyth
Claremont Garments	29	Howdon, Wallsend-on-Tyne
Claremont Garments	53	Peterlee
Claremont Garments	61	South Shields
Claremont Garments	71	West Auckland
Colony Country Store	37	Lindal-in-Furness
Dainty Supplies	69	Washington
Daleswear Factory Shop	30	Ingleton
Dannimac	41	Middlesbrough
Decoflora	72	Workington
Delcor Furniture	57	Seaton Delaval
Delta Outdoor Equipment	44	Newcastle upon Tyne
Dewhirst	3	Ashington
Dewhirst	54	Peterlee
Dewhirst	56	Redcar (Dormanstown)
Dewhirst	65	Sunderland
Durham Clothing	60	Shildon
Errington Reay (Bardon Mill Pottery)	5	Bardon Mill near Hexham
The Factory Bedding & Fabrics Shop	12	Carlisle
Factory Carpets and Factory Beds	6	Blaydon-on-Tyne
Factory Fabrics	7	Blaydon-on-Tyne
The Factory Shop	24	Egremont
Famous Fashion Discounts	63	Stockton-on-Tees

Index

The photographs on p. 6 show:
Dewhirst, Blyth; Linden Upholstery, Workington; Jacksons Landing, Hartlepool; Wynsors, Stockton; Famous Fashion Discounts, Stockton; Ward Arts & Crafty Warehouse, Gateshead; Dewhirst, Peterlee; Durham Clothing, Shildon; Claremont Garments, Peterlee.
The photograph on p. 7 is in Famous Fashion Discounts.